PERSEVERANCE, PROFANITY AND A POT OF GREASE

'Dick' 1917 aged twenty-one.

Maureen Carter

PERSEVERANCE, PROFANITY AND A POT OF GREASE

Author: Maureen Carter

National Library of Australia Cataloguing-in-Publication entry
Creator: Carter, Maureen, author.
Title: Perseverance, Profanity and a Pot of Grease/Maureen Carter.
ISBN: 9780994422002 (paperback)
Subjects: Australian fiction.
Dewey Number: A823.4

Book cover image title, 'Commiseration' produced by artist, Jennifer Marshall © Copyright 2014
www.lighthorseart.com.au

Published with the assistance of www.loveofbooks.com.au

Love of Books
Dream - Explore - Publish

Acknowledgements

I am deeply thankful to kind relatives who generously shared their memories and knowledge regarding the life of my estranged grandfather of whom this tale is broadly based.

I am also grateful to David Scott and Susanne Morris and other members of the Tamborine Mountain Writers Group who under their skilful guidance, encouraged me to write this story from true facts and folklore, plus a thank you to the staff at the Tamborine Mountain Library for their assistance, and Julie from Love of Books publications for her patience.

My appreciation also extends to talented artist, (Jennifer Marshall) for her most generous gift of the cover image titled, 'Commiseration.'

CONTENTS

PERSEVERANCE, PROFANITY

AND A POT OF GREASE

Prologue

"Well, I haven't seen my dad for six years but he's well-known throughout the Kimberley Region," young Jim bragged. "He can fix machinery, shoot dead-straight, tame and ride any horse, skin a bullock on the ground single-handed, and build a house. He can also black-smith, make a saddle and plait rawhide ropes." Teary-eyed he reminisced, "Even though he was a tough bugger, he was gentle with mum and us kids."

After an extra beer which was unusual for the camp's cook, Yankee George looked towards Jim. "Hey there son, I got something I ought to tell you, so listen up."

"What is it George?"

He didn't want to say too much, so continued cautiously, "By a strange co-incidence, it kinda happens that I knew your dad. We last met up four years ago when I was working in North Queensland."

"Well bugger me!" Jim uttered stunned. He had not seen his American father Dick, since the family's evacuation from the cattle station in the Kimberley Region.

"So, where is he living, George?"

"He's not there now, son - he never hangs around for long. He was talking about moving on, so he could be anywhere by now."

A dingo howled in the distance and Jim wondered if George could be his father. There was a certain likeness but casting his memory back, he remembered that his dad would be much younger than him and not as tall.

George enquired, "Did your mum tell you about the tucker bag incident involving him?"

"No, what happened?"

After revealing that important information, George added, "The last time I had contact with Dick, he was married again and this time to a relative of our Prime Minister."

Jim was intrigued. He decided if an opportunity arose, he would try to trace his father's whereabouts and confirm if the 'tucker bag incident' was true.

****

Chapter 1: WHERE'S MY DAD?

It was 1954 and Robert Menzies was the Prime Minister of Australia. Queen Elizabeth 11 and the Duke of Edinburgh had recently disembarked from the Royal Yacht 'Britannia' in Fremantle before heading to Sydney during their first Australian visit.

At that time Jim was fourteen years old and living in Western Australia. He worked with a gang of men constructing an inland road connecting Northampton to Carnarvon. Labouring under the blazing summer sun, converting two hundred and seventy miles of track into a highway proved a difficult task for a youngster.

The kangaroos and emus inhabiting that area had fled from the disruption, yet giant ant-hill sentries stood stoic above the scrub, confident their eerie structures would ward off any further intrusion to their territory. Then from above a rare scattering of gums, the Kookaburras raucous laughter rang out announcing to all native life the promise of rain. This would create havoc to the human trespassers and the outback would be their own again.

Thundering a rattle of death, Jim's heavy road-roller came to an abrupt stop and discovering a tree root caught in the axle, the boss shouted, "Righto blokes, we'll call it a day!" And the men chorused their agreement.

The sun began to set accompanied by cooler night air. Jim yawned and stretched his tired limbs then knelt to retrieve his utility knife lying on the ground. He held it tightly. How could he be so careless? It belonged to his father and he had kept it as a reminder. He sighed, yearning for his presence and replacing it deep in his trouser pocket, he gazed at the heavens wondering where his dad could be. *It's Gods own secret* came the sacred, quiet reply.

A pleasant scent of wattle and eucalypt was replaced by an enticing aroma from the camp's kitchen. Smirking, Yankee George teased the approaching men, "Hey guys, you're in for a great treat tonight! Rations are low but for you Aussies, I've grubbed together a true bush banquet of possum stew, spiced emu giblets and stale damper."

Winking at the men, the boss jibbed, "Yeah George? Well how about we catch a few wombats tomorrow and see what you can do with them!"

Before the cook could quip a reply, the boss had disappeared but the men knew his routine. On cue, he re-appeared with the beer-stash kept cool in the creek and behaving like Santa, gleefully handed the bottles out. The men's faces lit like excited children and clutching pocket knives, they cracked open their coldies to quench their immense thirst.

After a swift wash in the creek, kerosene lamps were lit before lashings of tucker were served and it was polished off with gusto following the hard day's yakka. But the

2

consumption of *strong* gassy beer soon resulted in a case of *strong*, windy indigestion.

For the boss, this conjured a mischievous idea for the night's entertainment. "Okay blokes!" he announced. "Give me your attention!" Silence fell over the camp as he continued, "It's time to start the night's competition and the lucky bugger who wins will be allowed off kitchen duties."

"Struth, what do we have to do to earn that?" came a stray comment.

Continuing, their boss kept a straight face, "Tonight, we're looking for the finest of gentlemen and well-bred of you all who can give us the most violent belch of wind. And I need to warn you, it must be from the mouth and not the other end!"

"Yeah... we'd need a bigger reward for that, hey boss?" came another response.

Eager to be accepted by the rough gang, young Jim raised his hand. Standing tall, he bent down to inhale a deep breath then rose to let go his burp of vulgarity.

"Good one son!" someone yelled.

Next, the boss followed suit with a pretty weak attempt, earning a thumb's down reaction from the audience. The other three were fairly darn good, but when Mighty Mick let rip his monster roar; it knocked them from their seats in shock. Howling with laughter, the men began the clean-up cracking jokes as they worked; their humour and mateship keeping spirits uplifted.

Before retiring for the night, they smoked tobacco in pipes or rolled cigarettes while seated around the dying embers of the fire telling tales that were either tallies or true-blue. And it was during a night like that, when Jim told the story about his father and in return, Yankee George shared a small portion of information regarding Jim's father's life in Queensland.

Three years later, Jim joined the Australian Army where he served twenty-eight years. Two of those years were spent in Malaya and two in Vietnam; in-between deployments, he transferred to the 2nd Light Horse Infantry. By another strange twist of fate, he later discovered that his dad had served in that same unit, fifty years earlier during the First World War.

While in the forces, a third event was to occur when travelling through the town of Stanthorpe, Queensland. He noticed the road sign to Texas and recalled his dad telling his mother; *if anything happens, I'll go back to Texas.* Overcome by nostalgia, he wondered if his father was living there and what he may be doing.

It was forty-seven years after his conversation with Yankee George when Jim finally found his answer surrounding his dad, Dick. It occurred while searching the world-wide internet.

******

Chapter 2: *JIM'S DAD 'DICK,' AND GRANDPA 'JULES'*

Jim's dad was known by the nickname of 'Dick,' and following his birth in 1896 in Missouri, America, a tornado struck that state causing widespread devastation. It killed many people, injured a large number more and left numerous others homeless. Luckily for Dick's family, their small town of German settlers was spared but five years later, a different type of disaster struck.

Dick was only five years of age when his mother died of tuberculosis. In desperation, Dick's pa, Jules left his sons in the joint care of their aunt and grandmother and while financially providing for them, the boys rarely saw their father again.

For Dick, this early experience left him with the impression that women raised children by themselves, carried out most of the chores and served their men-folk when they chose to appear. He also gained the notion that children were an inconvenience to their father unless their worth served him well.

Dick's pa, Jules, owned a lumber business in Kansas City and their home town of Concordia where he was also that area's Dentist. He was a suave and sophisticated man who always wore a suit and bow-tie and although seemingly respectable, his downfall was his womanising.

Left in a predicament after the death of his mother, Jules swiftly found a wife to care for his three sons, but following the birth of another boy, he began a secret affair with his assistant nurse.

Gossip in the small, deeply religious town travelled rapidly. It soon reached Jules first wife's brother, Mayor Jo Kuhlman who was waiting at his residence for their weekly meeting.

Alighting from his sulky before the Mayor's magnificent, federation style home, Jules grunted to a friendly Negro worker, "Make sure this goddamned horse is watered and tied securely or else!"

He strode in looking forward to discussing the town's latest news over a whisky and game of cards. But Jo was not in the parlour, instead, he found him sitting in his den in deep thought. He glanced up nodding towards a chair announcing solemnly, "Jules, I suggest you sit down before you hear this week's tidings."

But sensing rumour, he approached Jo curiously, whispering, "What is it?"

Jo reached for his pipe and held it upside down lighting its tobacco with a match. He turned it right side up, gave a quick suck and blew out the smoke, then with eyes creased in anger he spoke, "Unfortunately it involves you!"

Bewildered, Jules fell into his seat loosening his bow-tie waiting anxiously for what was to come.

Jo took a deep draw on his pipe followed by a strong puff declaring, "The latest rumour informs me that you've been having an affair with your assistant nurse." Then, with a look that could kill, he demanded, "I need to know if it's true!"

Stunned, Jules remained silent. He had known Jo a long time and knew of his high moral values but now caught out; he bowed his head, coughed uneasily and confessed, "It is indeed true....I cannot deny it... I don't know what came over me."

Jo rose from his chair shaking his head in disappointment and paced the floor twirling his handle-bar moustache. Finally, he halted, stood tall and lectured, "In this town, we hold our marriage vows sacred....I cannot believe you behaved in such a sinful way and tarnished our family's good name, linked through generations!"

Striding across the room again, he sucked deeper on his pipe and puffed slowly before clearing his throat. "I'm afraid there's no other option Jules - you'll have to leave this town and never return!"

Devastated at being banished, Jules acknowledged he had been a fool in not considering this outcome earlier. He would miss this town he was born in and spent his childhood but with high regard for Jo, he rose to his feet, looked him in the eye and shaking his hand, sadly confessed, "I'm sorry it's come to this Jo... I'm sure gonna miss you and this town."

Jules returned home, shattered. He sat alone in his study sipping whisky throughout the night. By dawn, the bottle lay empty by his side but his decision was made.

******

Chapter 3: *PUEBLO, COLORADO, U.S.A.*

Jules sold his business in Concordia before heading to Kansas City with his second eldest son, Dick. After inspecting his lumber yard in that town, he announced to its manager, "I can see that my eldest son, Delmar has been a good help to you during the past year, but now I need him myself. If you keep the business operating without him to my satisfaction, you can look forward to a healthy bonus come Christmas."

Jules appeared unconcerned at leaving his wife and two youngest sons behind in Missouri and following a meal at the railway restaurant, he boarded the hissing steam train with Delmar and Dick who revelled in their pa's attention, educating them on the railway and its network.

The train puffed its way through the countryside while Dick swayed to the constant movement of their carriage and click-clacking of train over rail. He sat by the window looking at the changing scenery and wildlife. When a large cattle ranch came into view, he watched in awe while cowboys on horses cracked whips through a cloud of dust, rounding up cattle into a yard. Yearning to be with them, he sighed when that scene was left behind.

Suddenly, he blinked in disbelief dropping down the sooty window. "Pa! Del! Look!" he shouted excitedly, "There's a real live Indian and it sure looks like he's hunting for animals!" The hunter was dressed in animal skins and carried a bow with a quiver of arrows draped over his shoulder as a male child tagged behind.

Their pa stated disapprovingly, "Listen to me, the both of you. Don't have anything to do with them red-skins. They're heathens!"

"How do you know that, Pa?" Dick asked.

"Mind your tongue and don't question me, son. I've heard of what they get up to, and I am warning you not to mix with their kind!"

Appalled at his attitude, Dick recalled the same negative stand toward Negro workers at his lumber yard.

The vehicle's rocking motion lulled them to sleep until woken by the blast of its whistle. The train decreased speed and then followed by a noisy screech of brakes, it halted with a long hiss of steam. Dick rubbed his bleary eyes, searching for the town's name board. "Welcome to Pueblo, Colorado," he read out loud.

They stepped onto the platform carrying heavy luggage and choking on pollution from the train. Abruptly, the guard's pea-whistle blew with a piercing shrill causing Dick to become disoriented and as throngs of people spilled onto the crowded platform, he was lost. Fearing abandonment, he searched in vain for his kin. "Dick, this way!" his father's voice boomed above the din, "Keep up with us and follow me!"

The boys set down their bags in an old hotel's foyer, sinking into plush chairs while their pa booked in. But irritated by musty smells of tobacco and alcohol, they walked across the room to view pictures on the back wall. Dick's eyes lit up nudging his brother, "Hey Del, take a look here. They're sketches of the town's outlaws wanted for goddamn capture.... If we caught one of those mean looking cads; we could end up with a huge reward!"

Delmar rolled his eyes, "Keep dreaming young buddy and you might just conjure up two guns and horses," he teased, "and while you're at it ...don't forget your big shiny Sherriff badge!"

Ignoring his sarcasm, Dick pointed to the front wall remarking, "Well now, take a look at this. It's a map of the city with a bit of information." He began to read out loud until his brother protested,

"I can read it myself, goof head!"

It stated;

This lively and prosperous city of Pueblo generates most of its wealth from steel, coal and gold mining industries. Located on the high, flat prairie, east of the foothills of the Rocky Mountains and south of Colorado Springs, this city is established on the banks of the confluence of the Arkansas River and Fountain Creek. The river, a major tributary of the Mississippi, has its initial basin in Colorado then flows into Kansas, Oklahoma and Arkansas. The river and its systems were the lifeblood for Native Americans who followed it for hunting and trapping.

The reference of Native Americans stirred Dick's sense of adventure and that night, he dreamt he rode a horse along

11

river banks to Indian tepees where he was welcomed by elders to join their hunt. He killed a boar and was made a hero but when the chief insists Dick marries his daughter, he refused. The offended elder ordered him killed then dodging their spears and arrows, Dick yelled, "No! No! Don't kill me!" ..... Abruptly he awoke, knocked by a shoe tossed at his head, then scornfully watched his brother settle smugly back to bed.

In the morning, the boys decided to explore the city while their father visited a gentlemen's club and despite it being a cold and gloomy day, they set off cheerfully, inhaling crisp morning air.

They wandered down a leafy tree-lined street gaping at stately-mansions when Delmar paused in front of the most magnificent one exclaiming, "Wow! How good would it be living in this?" He began to walk while sharing his day-dream... "Servants at your beck and call, grand parties with banquets, and pretty dames bickering at each other for the chance to dance with... ugh! Goddamn it! Jeepers!"

Dick laughed at his brother sprawled on the ground after thumping the lamp post, "You sure look *the dandy* now!" he taunted, "been drinking at your fancy party, have you?"

He stumbled to his feet, hollering, "If you think you're so darn smart, try to outrun me to the park!"

They raced towards its main entrance where they stood admiring its elaborate design. Its decorative iron gates were attached to pillars of granite under the fierce watch of gargoyles warding off acts of ill-will.

Greeted by bright music and a smell of coal steam, the youths curiously followed its trail which ended in a dazzle of colour. "It's a goddamn carousel," Del cried out, "and plum-darn spanking new!"

The beautiful construction rotated while excited children sat upon its wooden horses and chariots that dipped and bobbed to music. Delmar asked its sweat and grease smeared operator, "Sir, how does it work?"

Flattered at the opportunity to flaunt his knowledge, the friendly, grey haired man replied proudly, "The mechanism is operated by a steam engine and the organ music is emitted from a perforated cylinder that works similar to a pianola."

They moved aside and catching a mouth-watering aroma wafting from the hot-dog stand, hungrily took their place in line. After washing it down with cold soda, Dick tugged his brother's shirt. "Jeepers Del," he whispered, "take a look at that little busker heading our way."

The vividly dressed clown wore a wide grin but stood boldly in their path. Snatching Delmar's hat, he waved it around to reveal it empty and with a tap of wand, pulled out a toy white rabbit while they stood entranced. Then, the performer held out a nickel on the palm of his hand and after clapping hands together, opened them to show it had disappeared. He then placed his hand beside Dick's right ear where the coin reappeared, and pushing it in that ear; made it look like it had fallen out of his other ear.

The lads gasped in surprise and were about to ask how it was done, when he showed them his empty hands again and plunging one in Delmar's trouser pocket, withdrew a large and colourful, silk scarf. They were still gaping when the clown bowed and disappeared among the crowd.

Stunned by the quick departure, an unpleasant thought jolted Delmar. He yelled, "Dick, that buffoon has goddamned stolen my wallet!"

They gave chase and searching a toilet block nearby, found the clown's discarded costume. "That rotten scoundrel must have headed for the river," Delmar shouted angrily and racing in that direction, found the man peeping from behind a tree. As they approached, he scrambled for a boat moored at the river's edge, but nabbed him before he jumped on board.

"What do you want? Leave me alone!" he cried in fright.

"Not before you hand over my wallet!" Delmar roared, grabbing him by the throat.

"What do you mean? I haven't got your stupid wallet!" he squawked.

"I know you're the one who stole it!" Delmar haughtily declared, "because you're wearing the same goddamned shoes."

They pinned him down while Dick retrieved his brother's possession, then grabbing him by the seat of his pants; they threw him in the river. "Now clever magician, watch yourself disappear!" Delmar sniggered.

Laughing, they returned to the park's entrance where the street-car was ready to depart. "Jeepers Del, the day turned out to be darn good after all," Dick commented happily seated at his side.

"I sure do reckon, young buddy, and pa missed out on a real goddamn, dippin' time!"

Delmar informed their pa about the day's adventure after boarding the train the following day. Dick sat by the window staring out as others talked and enthralled by the landscape, he decided at the first opportunity, he would live a life offering freedom to roam.

******

Chapter 4:   STOCKTON, CALIFORNIA, U.S.A.

They arrived in Stockton, California where their pa became the proud owner of another lumber business but he was distant to his sons, spending much of his time drinking and playing cards at a gentleman's club.

The brothers were not naïve - they knew beautiful women were available there for the men's pleasure and wished they were twenty-one years old so they could accompany their pa. Delmar would be eligible well before Dick who feared being left out when that time came.

The brothers lived in the barn attached to the saw-mill while their pa resided in a small cabin behind the office. Apart from Sunday dinner, the only time he spared with them was to bark an order or grumble about their work.

"Our goddamn horses are better company than pa," Dick grizzled to his brother. "He feeds and clothes us but we're more like slaves than sons, and he never includes us in his life." Tearfully he added, "If I lose your company Del, I'll go just plum-darn crazy!"

"I know what you mean, young buddy, but you better get used to the idea. I can't wait to turn twenty-one; at least *I'll* have a better life then."

It was 1912, and Dick's sixteenth birthday was nearing. He imagined his pa presenting him with a gift and cake and playing a game of chess together, but those thoughts were interrupted by his sudden command, "Hey there sons, come on over here! I've just received the latest newspaper and it seems the rumour is true."

"What is it Pa?" Dick asked.

"Well, I'm afraid it doesn't sound too good. It's about that fancy ship, The Titanic." He began to read; *News-scoop......Titanic Tragedy!*

The British passenger liner RMS Titanic, carrying two thousand, two hundred and twenty-four people, has collided with an iceberg in the North Atlantic Ocean and sunk. She was on her maiden voyage from Southampton in England, to New York City. Rescuers are on their way and we'll update you with the latest news as soon as it comes to us. Make sure to buy the next edition!

Shocked, their pa bowed his head. "Dear Lord God, we pray they all survive and if not, then God rest their poor souls." He sadly shook his head becoming angry, "And we were told it was so goddamn unsinkable!"

After hearing that news, Dick gratefully accepted his own lot in life at that time.

Regardless of the world's disasters, the town of Stockton was bustling with activity and their thriving business kept the boys occupied. At the end of most days, they lost themselves in a world of their own reading novels from their pa's collection.

17

Dick discovered that since the mid-nineteenth century, Stockton had become an important place of supply and departure for prospective gold miners. The San Joaquin River flowed to San Francisco and the river's depth and width, created a natural inland seaport for the town. It also held an extensive network of waterways, fished and navigated for centuries by the Miwok and Yakut Indians. The Miwok lived in the central valley among the delta's waterways and the Yakut, in the north-east area of Stockton along the Calaveras River and up into the foothills following the river's South Fork.

Inspired by the native's culture, Dick then read about the Siskiyou Trail - an ancient footpath leading through the Sacramento Valley, over the Cascades and on to Oregon. Yearning for adventure; Dick tested his brother's future intentions, "Hey Del, how about we leave this goddamn place and go check out that Siskiyou Trail together?"

"Well, I'm reading a book," he replied annoyed, "It's called - you're a big goof head and plum-darn crazy!"

Another night, Dick read a Mark Twain novel and racing through it to the last page, he thought of a more appropriate idea. "Hey, Del, how about we explore the river by raft?" It was then; his brother's eyes lit up with interest.

The next day, they gathered light weight poles from their yard and constructed a crude platform by lashing the poles together with twine. After scavenging four lidded, empty liquor barrels from the hotel, they attached them below the corners of the platform creating buoyancy for their raft.

Another pole formed the mast and a bed sheet became its sail, tied for easy release. Then Delmar stood back to admire their work. "Now ain't that just the greatest raft, you ever cast your eye on!" he proudly declared.

Apprehensively, they pushed their raft into the river. It floated, so they climbed on board and shoved off from shore. "Yee-Ha! We did it!" Dick hollered, drifting away.

In the middle of the river, they were greeted by a variety of craft from the most basic canoe to the grand old lady of them all - the Paddle Wheeler. The sparkling water held a bounty of sea life below its depth and the fishing boats that passed, overflowed with an abundance of catch.

They watched in amazement as the landscape changed rapidly from low banks to high cliffs, and thick forest to sandy beaches under a clear, blue sky.

The brightly coloured stalls of a noisy market place littered the shoreline but the voices muted in the distance as their raft sped with the fast flow of the river.

While exhilarated with freedom, the lads lost all sense of time until hunger pangs jolted Dick back to reality, suggesting, "Hey Del, how about a bit of grub?"

"Sure thing!" he replied, but searching for it, he became worried. "Well, I have the water but where's our food?"

Rummaging under the folded sail, Dick teased, "Jeepers Del," I think it must have fallen through a goddamn crack!"

"What?" he hollered in disbelief. "Trust you to lose it, you goof head!"

Amused, Dick watched his brother's face seethe annoyingly until confessing, "It ain't lost... It was here all along, you bigger goof!"

No sooner had they polished it off, when they were startled by a horn blast from a paddle wheeler bearing down on them from behind. "Holy, shit!" Del shouted, "Let out the goddamn sail! We need it now!"

The raft gained speed as the sail was freed but the huge vessel approached rapidly. Unable to divert their direction, they were at the mercy of the wind which blew them straight ahead and although paddling furiously, another horn blast almost knocked them overboard. Then faced with no choice, they jumped into the river and swam for their lives.

A loud crack rang out and they looked back to see their craft split apart. They had escaped the fierce impact, but as they desperately tried to swim ashore, the current pulled them away. When near to exhaustion, Delmar spat out a mouthful of water, yelling, "Follow me!"

He changed course and angled to the bank instead of swimming directly to it. His idea worked and reaching dry land, they flopped onto the shoreline where they lay regaining strength.

Dick slowly lifted his head and looking at his brother lying still, called anxiously, "Del, are you alright?" No answer came and he dragged himself closer listening for his breath. There was no sound or movement, so he frantically grabbed his wrist to feel a pulse.

"Boo!" his brother shouted opening his eyes.

Dick fell back yelling, "You, big goof head!"

They were wrestling playfully, when startled by a stocky, grey haired man who appeared from the woods. He caught his breath uttering, "Are you two young'uns okay?"

They nodded smiling.

"You're both lucky to be alive and you can thank your dear Lord Jesus for that!" He lectured, "I was enjoying a view of the river from the hillside until I saw your predicament, and you near darn gave me a heart attack."

"Sorry, sir," they replied together.

Grinning, he joked, "Now I wonder what you two young'uns names could be? I don't suppose you're the famous Tom Sawyer and Huckleberry Finn, huh?"

"I reckon that's who we tried to be," Delmar answered.

"Where do you live? If it's not too far, I'll get you to your kin."

"We're from a lumber business in Stockton," said Delmar.

"Well I do declare, our Lord works in mysterious ways, because that's where I'm heading. I work for a big establishment there run by the Holt Brothers."

After climbing on board his sulky tethered by the roadside, the youths entertained him with the entire day's events.

During this time in Stockton, the Holt Brothers produced machinery for track-laying. Later, in the First World War, the invention was redesigned for the production of bullet-proof tanks by the British Army aiding Britain to win the war. Unknown to Dick then, he was to play a small part in that same victory.

Time flew by and soon celebrations were made for Delmar's twenty-first birthday and induction to his father's club. Dick was left on his own most nights and he became increasingly restless. Afraid his pa would prevent him leaving, he quietly packed his bags, placed a note on his bed and set off by paddle wheeler to begin a new life in San Francisco.

******

Chapter 5: SAN FRANCISCO, U.S.A.

San Francisco was a dynamic city by 1915 following a full recovery from the devastating earthquake and flood almost a decade earlier. Situated at the entrance to one of the world's best natural harbours, it developed as a centre for maritime trade with completion of the Panama Canal. Proving to the world its potential, it hosted the Panama-Pacific International Exposition from February to December of that year.

The centrepiece of this mighty enterprise was the Tower of Jewels located on the city's northern shore among impressive fountains, gardens and commercial exhibits. Covered in star shaped gems, it sparkled in sunlight throughout the day while at night, was illuminated by fifty electric searchlights. The United States Government authorised commemorative coinage and postage stamps to be issued to celebrate the grand event.

On arrival in this vibrant city, Dick obtained employment at the dockyards and although physically draining, found the work no more difficult than working for his pa. He was well-paid with each Sunday free and following his city exploits, he was led to the local park by the stirring sound of the navy brass-band's performance.

Upon the return of spring, the old oaks burst with new foliage and the birds sang happily. The rose garden bloomed with new life and its fragrance filled the air. Dick was inhaling its scent when he was struck by a sight too good to be true, and rubbing his eyes to prove it was no delusion, he blinked them open as he stood entranced, ogling a young, pretty female wearing ringlets of long blonde hair.

Assuming an air of confidence, he sauntered across to the bench where she sat licking an ice cream and lured further by it dripping from her red lips, he boldly sat by her side.

She glanced at him fluttering her eye lashes.

He gulped nervously stammering, "Does that ice cream taste as good as it looks?"

To his surprise, she offered it flirting, "Have a lick and find out!"

He declined respectfully, "Ma'am, before I go sharing my germs, I ought to make it right and introduce myself first.... I'm Dick."

"I'm sorry if I seem brazen," she admitted, "my name's Valencia but you can call me Val."

After three hours of non-stop chatter, Dick told her, "I feel like I've known you all my goddamn life."

"That's odd! I feel the same."

"Well, maybe we should meet up again next Sunday?" he suggested.

"That sounds fine by me," she smiled.

Throughout the week his thoughts were filled day-dreaming about her attractiveness while longing for Sunday to come. When it did, he found her waiting at the same spot.

Twirling a parasol above her head, her frilly apron skirt was worn daringly at calf-length and the prudish cameo clasping her blouse, failed miserably to hide her ample cleavage.

Valencia was excited to see Dick heading her way. His charming blue eyes, tanned skin and strong body captivated the seventeen-year-old arousing feelings she had never known.

Suddenly, their eyes locked. Then kissing Valencia's hand, he raised her up to stroll the path together while talking incessantly. She confided, "You know, my life reads like yours but the other way around.

"What do you mean?"

"I was very young when my *father* died and *my mum* is more interested in her life than mine." She explained, "I had a good education until last year. That's when the money ran out because of *her* drinking and it created a lot of problems." She frowned, "And I should warn you that she won't approve of our friendship - she constantly reminds me that in one year's time, I'm to marry our wealthy old neighbour who promised to take care of us both."

Concerned by that news, Dick drew her protectively close. "Don't worry, honey. As long as I'm around, I'll make darn sure it never happens!"

Valencia felt supported by his pledge as they wandered to a secluded area by the river. It was late and under the setting sun, she yielded in his strong embrace and then tilting her face towards his, they become lost in a lingering kiss. Unfastening her blouse, his arousal increased and they passionately made love for the first time.

In soothing warmth of his arms, she tearfully pleaded, "I don't want to go home - I want to stay with you forever!"

Momentarily dumbfounded, he admitted, "Well... I've been planning to check out Australia for a while but was waiting for a goddamn fool reason." He hesitated before suggesting, "So, why don't we stowaway together?" Then jolted by a memory, his eyes lit up, "And there happens to be goddamn ship leaving in that direction in the morning!"

Taken by surprise, there was silence as Valencia's mind ticked over, "Well... my life is so unbearably dull.... No one really cares whether I live or die." She smiled mischievously, "But that sounds extra wild to me, so why not?"

She wanted to feel needed and loved and when he kissed and encircled her, his muscular body and manly scent affected her in a new, strange way and she wished to stay with him from now on.

Encouraged by her enthusiasm, he began a plan. "We could meet at this old oak tree at five in the morning. Wear a dark coat and bring a rug and whatever you can carry. But we must be aboard the boat by five thirty - that's when the sailors have breakfast."

She frowned, "But Dick, where could we hide?"

"The cargo-hold is a sure darn perfect place and I know where we can enter."

"Well, that sounds fine by me!"

"But don't forget, we must meet at five, so don't be late."

"I'll try my best to make it Dick, so *please* don't go without me!"

He walked her home with his arm wrapped around her and they kissed and parted.

Following a sleepless night, Dick arrived at the tree early and with no sign of Valencia by ten past five, he began to pace. When a cuckoo bird called, he sensed an omen to depart. Then before he lost hope, Valencia appeared suddenly, carrying a heavy load. He ran to help and after tucking her hair into his cap, they headed to the dock and boarded the ship.

Their lives together had begun.

******

Chapter 6: THE STOWAWAYS

Dick and Valencia arrived safely at their hideout in the cargo-hold where they huddled together in a corner until cranking engines heralded the ship's imminent departure.

After creating a warm bed from blanket and clothing, Valencia announced, "I've brought a bucket to wash in and one for *you know what*....... and I've just spied our separate area."

"What do you mean by our separate area?" Dick asked disappointedly.

"It's where we do our *other business*," she explained, embarrassed.

"Jeepers honey, you think of everything," he uttered feeling like an idiot. He then bragged, "Well, I've brought enough food for three days but after that, *I'll* be the one to go on the hunt!"

While the huge ship groaned and creaked as it steamed through the water, Dick examined their musty, cramped conditions. Crawling towards a dark object, his eyes widened, exclaiming, "It's a full cask of drinking water! - So *now* who's the goddamn smartest?" Soon, he scowled, "But it's so gloomy in here, we could go stir-crazy!"

"Well, I brought candles and matches," Valencia chirped and as she lit one, it created a warm ambience. "Now, it seems kinda romantic," she huskily murmured. He embraced her soft body, brushing her neck with his warm breath and she melted in his arms. The pleasant scent of her hair aroused him and tantalising her with his moist kiss, it increased in strength. They tore at each other's clothes feverishly and after lying together impassioned, drifted off to sleep.

Awakening from a long slumber, they consumed their first meal aboard – bottled soda water and sandwiches; Valencia gasping in disgust when a rat ran off with the crumbs. Later, the couple emerged on deck, stretching their legs and bathing in sunshine from a secluded area while the ship's crew had lunch.

By the third day, their supplies were depleted and with stomachs grumbling, Dick was forced to risk roaming the ship for food.

At midnight, he arrived to the galley where he gathered supplies but alarmed by approaching feet, he dashed into the cold room closing the door. An intense chill set in and he gripped the handle but to his distress, it fell off in his hand. Profanities misted from his mouth in a useless attempt to replace it and numb from cold, he no longer cared if caught. He cried out fearfully, kicking the door but no one came.... It was then, he spied a meat hook but with stiff fingers, they refused to grip. He blew warm breath on them and gained feeling but when grabbing the hook, it frosted to his hand. Rubbing it against his clothes, the hook loosened. He picked the lock, the door swung open and then securing his stash, staggered out.

Craving Valencia's warm body, Dick swiftly returned to the hideout where stumbling over her sleeping form, he collapsed by her side. But snapped awake by his icy arm, she shrieked in terror until his swift hand muted her cries. "It's only me, Val," he shuddered, "help me get warm!" He then told her of his near-death experience while she comforted him in her arms. "Hell, and all this on my goddamn nineteenth birthday!" he concluded, needy of more sympathy.

"Oh, my poor darling, and I can't even bake you a cake!" she teased and tickling him playfully, it soon led to another night of heated bliss.

It didn't take long for boredom to set in while limited to a game of cards but during the second week, there was a drastic change. The weather had taken a turn for the worst, and as the ship rolled from side to side and howling winds increased, Valencia became nervous, frightened, then sea sick. Looking as fragile as a china doll, she weakly asked, "What if the ship sinks and we drown?"

Dick puffed out his chest, feigning bravado, "You'll be fine, honey. This kinda thing happens on high seas, besides.... you've got me to save you!" But his reassurance didn't work - she staggered to the private area and unromantically, threw-up.

The following day, the sea had calmed. Valencia needed sunshine and crept warily outside. When feeling better and about to return, she gasped in surprise as an ominous shadow cast over her. She swung around wearing a look of terror.

The young sailor attempted to calm her, soothing, "Sorry, to frighten you ma'am....I promise I won't say anything and if you need supplies, I could fetch them for you."

She took advantage of his kindness, replying, "Thank God for your mercy! I haven't eaten for days and was about to end it all!"

His handsome face creased with concern, "Hey, there's no need to do a fool thing like that.... I can help a damsel in distress." After checking no one in sight, he added, "I'll tap twice when I have supplies, but please get back inside - someone else may not feel the same."

Over-hearing the conversation, Dick praised her as she re-appeared, "Wow honey, you should be an actress on the stage!" But his face soon changed to a frown of jealousy, considering what to do if the guy had romantic ideas.

The young man did come back with provisions announcing in an attractive, deep voice, "By the way, my name is Chad. What's yours?"

"Call me Val."

Mystified he asked, "Why are you running away?"

"How long before we reach land?" she asked, changing the subject.

"We're just short of four weeks to the Philippine Islands... but if you feel cold and lonely, I could keep you company in there?"

"I'm doing fine on my own, thank you," she kindly asserted.

"Well, I'm mighty glad to hear you're okay, darlin'," he replied undeterred, "but I'll check on you each day until we reach port." He winked and left.

Dick greeted Valencia with a broad smile. "You're just too goddamn smart, honey! I didn't need to thump him yet and, I don't have to scrounge like a goddamn rat anymore." He then hugged and kissed her playfully.

While Dick remained hidden below, Chad continued to visit each day with ample supplies, behaving like a gentleman. It was during the last night when Dick was asleep that Chad knocked unexpectedly. Valencia opened the hatch as he announced, "In the morning, we make port for six days but take care leaving the ship. And darlin'," he added gently, "It sure would make my day, if we could meet up while we're there." He pressed his contact details into her hand and kissed it.

Valencia knew she could not fulfil his wish and despite being flattered by his advance, replied tactfully, "Chad, all I can say is; that if it's meant to be, then I'm sure it will happen."

Dick and Valencia knew Manila was in sight when alerted by sounds of increased activity in the morning. "Jeepers, I can't wait to set foot on land again," Dick grinned excitedly.

"And I can't wait for a warm bath and soft bed," Valencia dreamily remarked.

Suddenly, an announcement boomed from outside, "Prepare to land!" They heard heavy footsteps scurrying to tie down the ship as it slowed its engines, gradually thumping to a halt. But for the frustrated couple, it would be nightfall before they could make a safe escape.

When darkness fell after what seemed like an eternity, Dick instructed, "It's time to put on our dark coats. Follow me carefully and make sure your hair is tucked into the cap." He listened intently before cautiously emerging. They reached the gangway and made it swiftly to the dock when Valencia let out a gasp - her cap fell off, exposing her long blonde tresses....

"Stop...!"- Rang out in the still night, halting them in their tracks.

"Run!" Dick hollered, and they took off until the sound of running feet from behind disappeared. Then Dick halted and put down the bags, scooped Valencia in his arms and twirled her round and around until so dizzy, they fell to the ground, laughing.

******

Chapter 7: MANILA, PHILIPPINE ISLANDS

They booked into the nearest hotel and after a thorough soak and scrub, climbed into a bed of pure luxury.

Dick announced over breakfast, "Today, I'll look for work at the docks and if I'm lucky, it won't be long before we move on to Australia and get married."

Relieved by his promise of marriage, Valencia vowed, "I'll always love you Dick and I'm mighty glad I met you."

Dick's previous dockyard experience proved valuable and he was immediately employed. He boasted to Valencia after the third day, "My buddies have half accepted me already and after tomorrow, I'll wear their final seal of approval."

"What's that Dick? It's not some sort of secret society or something, is it?"

"Jeepers honey, it's not that exciting. It's kinda like an initiation into their union by testing your pain level."

"But I don't want you to get hurt.... I need you!"

"Don't worry. I intend being around a long time and in another six weeks, we should have enough money saved to start our married life in Australia."

After returning late the next day, he proudly displayed his new tattoo titled; 'Manila, P.I.' "It's all done, Val," he told her, "but the strange thing is; that at the sight of blood, the guy who was *my witness* fell down flat in a goddamn faint!"

She spluttered a laugh, he tickled her sides and when she burst into hysterics, he carried her off to bed. There, she gained the upper hand until he cried out, "Honey, I'm in pain - go easy on me!" When her brow creased with concern, he added, "I'm only joking - your face looks kinda cute when I'm seeking attention." He then grabbed her again and kissing her passionately, made love.

The next day, Valencia's loneliness set in and she decided to visit him at work. Nervously, she entered the street, yet stares from strangers speaking a foreign language dispelled her confidence. Then with a deep breath, she bravely joined the crowd of people, mules and carts heading towards the bay side.

The sight of squalid living conditions surrounding her was depressing but children playing happily, lifted her spirits when arriving at spicy food markets scattered by the bay's shore where bags of rice and tropical fruit were displayed under shade and vendors offered reams of colourful cloth. Bamboo furniture momentarily held her interest but when nearing a stall of woven baskets, a rooster's crow shrieked out from behind and as she stumbled against a cage, more poultry joined in, bantering loudly.

The commotion attracted other hawkers who circled like a mob of hungry vultures; one man begging, "You lady, buy *two* ducks, I charge you *one*....Not many peso, very cheap!"

"I'm not interested in buying," she cringed scurrying away but trays of seafood blocked her escape. The stench of dead fish made her queasy and dried octopus dangled in her face.

Then moving aside, she gasped in horror at a display of cured piglets with a sprig of herbs protruding from their mouths. Yet before clearing all stalls, there came a shout....

"You not get better deal, I make sure!"

The persistent man selling ducks reappeared exposing stained, buck teeth and pleading, "For you lady; I have four yum-yum rats.... Not many peso, very cheap!"

Valencia now ran towards the docks where sniffing tar fumes, she peacefully watched men apply a coat of its concoction to the wharfs timbers. Later, she searched for Dick and although glimpsing his face, a netted haul of cargo blocked him from sight.

Meanwhile.... *Chad* was standing around the corner when he saw Valencia. Overjoyed by the notion, she had come to meet *him,* he threw down his cigarette and headed her way, but halted abruptly when a voice of authority shouted, "There she is!"

Suddenly, a lawman grabbed her arm. She yelled indignantly, "Leave me alone! Let go of me!" But her cries were in vain as she was dragged away.

A witness identified her as the female seen escaping from the ship five days earlier and although ordered to return home, she showed complete loyalty to Dick by not implicating him. Sobbing hysterically, she asked for pen and paper. "Please make sure this note is delivered to my friend who I met *after* I arrived here. He needs to know what's happened." It was delivered to the hotel where belongings were gathered.

When Dick came home, he tore open the letter and reading it in disbelief, his world shattered around him. Unable to rescue her, he was left distraught and frustrated with an overwhelming dilemma - should he return to America and work out a way for them to be together - or should he fulfil his dream of travelling on to Australia?

The sun had arisen signalling the birth of a new day when Dick sucked the last dregs from a mug of strong coffee. He decided Australia was where he would head.

Meanwhile.... Chad was feeling optimistic regarding his future with Valencia. He recalled her words - *if it's meant to be, then I'm sure it will happen.* Destiny had stepped in and she was forced to return on his ship to America. And he was determined that no matter what her circumstance, he would make her his bride.

******

Chapter 8: CAIRNS, NORTH QUEENSLAND, AUSTRALIA

Dick disembarked from the steamship 'Changsha' that carried him as a stowaway from the Philippine Islands. No sooner had he set foot on land, when he saw someone eyeing him suspiciously, so he took off without looking back.

The hot sun emerged from behind clouds and his steaming body turned his clothing into wet rags. Exhausted and lonely, he sat in shade of coconut palms fanning his face with his cap. Squinting towards the glare of ocean, he recalled advice given from a San Francisco sailor - *If you want a ranch of your own, then Australia is the place to go. The land is free, the animals cheap, and there's gold in every creek.*

He was alone in a strange land, deeply missing Valencia's friendship and in a mood of depression, he wiped a tear. *Bright company and cold ale ought to fix my blues,* he thought, *but I'll need to exchange my goddamn money first!* Sniffing a fragrance of Frangipani; he stood up, then walking a tree-lined street of Poinciana blooms, he continued towards town with more optimism.

He emerged from the town's bank waving flies from his face and peering down the quiet road. A hotel stood at each corner and he was wondering which was the best; when a Cobb and Co. Coach pulled up to the nearest and as passengers spilled into it, he followed.

Dick felt comfortable chatting among these friendly people in the small town of Cairns, North Queensland. But exposing his intention to work in *their* Outback, the newly arrived Yank became *their* focus for amusement.

"Gee-wiz mate, so you want to go out west?" one man asked. "Well, watch out for those savage aborigines. They're worse than your bloody Indians. They're not only scalp hunters but bloody cannibals as well!"

"And struth mate," another added, "Don't be too quick to cool down in those tempting billabongs. The bloody big crocs will snap you in half; that's if the flies and mosquitoes don't get you first!" Then, shaking salt on his steak, spoke louder, "And crikey mate, don't be fooled by those dopey looking dingoes and 'roos. Before you can strike a light, they'll have a bloody go at you too!"

Tired of their taunts, Dick finished his drink and left to check out town before nightfall but he was not impressed. He stood watching kangaroos graze quietly on the edge of the road when a large buck came bounding towards him, fronting him with raised fists. Dick turned and ran; glancing back to find the animal had disappeared.

He sat on a park bench chasing flies with his cap and observing a spiky ant-eater poking for prey, he questioned his decision to stay, *what goddamn force led me to this God forsaken place? To experience work on a ranch, I'll need to live in a more secluded area. And goddamn it, I still miss Val..... I should go back and track her down.... But jeepers,* he sighed, *I'm here now so I'll give it one more goddamn week*!

He was tucking into a roast dinner at the hotel, washing it down with cold beer when a rough character sidled up. Dick turned his head to avoid ridicule but the man sat down beside him. "G'day cobber!" he cheerfully greeted, taking off his broad-brimmed hat and wiping his brow. "I heard at the bar grape vine that you're interested in a job as a station hand. Is that right?"

Surprised, Dick grinned, "Yeah pal, I sure am."

"Well, I happen to know of a bloke who owns a cattle station near Winton and he's looking for someone who's an all-rounder. I've just placed his details on the notice board at the mail office across the road. You could send a telegram from there if you're interested."

Dick beamed and shook the man's hand. "I'm mighty thankful to you sir."

The work involved horse and cattle handling, mending miles of fencing and many other odd jobs. A fair wage with board and keep was offered and training would be provided to the right person.

Two days later, a return telegram arrived. Dick's hands trembled unfolding the note and discovering good news, hollered, "Yee-Ha! At least, I've got a goddamn job!"

******

Chapter 9: *WINTON, QUEENSLAND*

The outback town of Winton is situated on the Great Artesian Basin and is serviced by the Diamantina River's off-streams. It's main industries were sheep and cattle-raising and this area made headline news during 1894 when Dagworth Station's wool shearing shed was burned down along with seven others in the district. This was part of a protest held by shearers regarding work conditions. A man implicated, was later found deceased along with the remains of a dead sheep at a nearby billabong known as 'Combo Waterhole.'

The following year a Sydney solicitor and poet, Banjo Patterson, stayed at Dagworth Station located sixty-three miles north-west of Winton. Inspired, after listening to the tune 'Craiglea,' played by a musician at that station and then visiting the billabong; he wrote an ode. And although those *original* lyrics held undertones of socialism, it was the First Ballad sung of Australia's latter, unofficial national anthem, 'Waltzing Matilda.' It was performed by Sir Robert Ramsay at a dinner held at Winton's North Gregory Hotel with the Premier of Queensland in the audience.

Dick reached Winton after travelling about six hundred miles south-west of Cairns by Cobb and Co. Coach and a weather-worn man supported by a walking stick, greeted him cheerfully, "G'day young fella! I'm Fred, your boss. Hop aboard the sulky and we'll be at the station in no time."

After arriving one hour later, Fred called out to three aborigines who approached them. The natives appeared wary of Dick and recalling the horror story told at the hotel in Cairns, he held the same feelings about them. "These men are my trusted workers," Fred told Dick. "They'll show you what you need to know, and I'll explain what needs to be done after we've all had tucker."

Dick confided during supper, "I aim to own a ranch myself one day, but I ain't sure about this goddamn isolation!"

"Well, young mate, although Australia is about the same size as your United States, only a third of it is habitable and our rainfall run-off is only about a sixth of where you come from." He shook his head. "Nah, us poor buggers have it tougher than you Yanks, and we've too many blasted droughts, floods and bushfires. But if you're a fair dinkum worker and use your nous; you could make a good living when the weather is kind, that is, if you can cope with the loneliness."

"But what about all that goddamn gold in the creeks?" Dick asked disappointedly, "I was told it's found everywhere!"

Fred laughed, "Well young fella, when you're my age, you learn to take those bloody exaggerated tales with a grain of salt. A bloke can waste his whole life looking for the big nugget and die wearing rags on his back." He leaned closer to add, "But if you prove your worth, young mate, this place could be yours one day!"

42

Dick was stunned by the generous offer, replying, "Well, I'm mighty grateful to you sir. I'll do my best, and not let you down!"

Dick grew to love the job, discovering the shy natives were friendly and through them and his boss, he gained valuable knowledge of bushmanship. At night, when seated around the campfire, Fred told exciting or amusing tales about his droving days. Dick was so enthralled; he hoped to enjoy that experience himself eventually.

One morning, when the boss rang the bell for smoko, Dick arrived sweating from his labour. The old man pointed to his horses with pride, remarking, "These Walers are strong and fast. They were bred by the early settlers to cope with our harsh environment. If times are tough, they can go without food and water for days. They're also very intelligent and have a calm temperament." Then he looked at Dick affectionately adding, "I notice you have a love for them and out here, a man needs a horse of his own, so go choose one for yourself, young mate."

Dick's eyes widened causing his boss to chuckle before urging, "Now, go on and pick one out!"

He selected a young horse named 'Wally' who fondly nudged Dick while he stroked its head.

After six months Dick yearned for company and gaining a break from work, he packed his swag and set off on Wally to attend a horse race at Longreach; about one hundred and twelve miles south-east of Winton and named after the *long reach* of the Thompson River.

The dusty track was easy to travel while galloping under cool, wintry skies and the few passing folk, dipped their hats or waved.

Dick was crossing a shallow gully when his ears pricked suddenly....A strange noise of clanging metal beat in time to the sound of tramping feet, and then from around a bend, an odd character emerged. A rug-roll was strung over his shoulder, pots and pans hung loose from his trouser braces and corks dangled from a tatty hat, pulled low. Then halting in surprise, the weather-beaten man raised his face. "G'day mate!" he greeted happily, "do ya fancy joining me for billy tea?"

Surprised by his friendliness Dick eagerly answered, "I sure would like that, pal!" He dismounted from his horse to shake his hand. "By the way, my name is Dick."

"You can call me whatever you like, but don't call me late for breakfast," the skinny tramp smirked.

Bewildered by the odd statement, Dick gathered kindling for a fire and once it was lit, the long bearded chap placed the billy to boil, tossing in a gum leaf. Then sweating heavily, he groaned as he bent to sit on a log asking, "So, you must be from up Winton way, young fella? - Now tell me; have ya ever crossed paths with that bloody weird Min-Min Light?"

"I'm sorry pal, but I ain't a clue as to what you're talking about," Dick confusingly answered, "I've only been in Australia for a short while."

"Arr.... I thought you talked funny; so, you wouldn't know about anything here at all, would ya?"

Dick felt uneasy by the tramp's hillbilly manner but relaxed when handed a tin mug of tea and sniffing its enticing aroma, settled back in comfort on a tree stump, listening to the tale unfold.

"Most people from around Winton or Boulia have heard about it.... I've seen it a few times in my travels and it still puts the wind up me!"

Moaning painfully, he changed his position on the log and after clearing his throat, spat on the ground before continuing, "But I'll never forget the first time I saw it... I was heading to Boulia on dusk... 'cause you don't last long walking through the day in summer.... When suddenly, it came out of the blue - a real creepy light!... I thought it was the moon but it was too close, and then it began to bob back and forward behind me."

"Was that after you had a few swigs of rum?" Dick interrupted.

"No mate!" He replied indignantly, picking a stray hair from his mouth. "I swore off that many years ago. It was fair dinkum, I swear! ....Anyway, I kept walking but it wouldn't go away. It scared the crap out of me; that's for sure! I ran as fast as my old legs were able, but it made fun of me by moving ahead as if in a race. I was exhausted and couldn't escape so I tried being friendly and talked to it."

Dick coughed, stifling a laugh. "So, you actually *talked* to the light?"

"Yeah, that's what I just told you!" he snapped. "So, I asked it; what is it like being a light? And it began to bob up and down real fast as if laughing at me."

Abruptly, Wally let out a high-pitched whinny and Dick, unable to contain his mirth, burst into hysterics and then rose to leave.

Offended, the old traveller shouted, "Don't you want to hear the end of it?"

"You made my day pal, but I need to make night-camp closer to Longreach," Dick replied adding with a wink, "I don't want that goddamn Min-Min Light to put the wind up me!"

Eucalyptus scent infused the air as he rode by an unusual area of large gum trees, and then halted his horse to inspect their height. "Jeepers, that looks like a koala up there!" he uttered, amazed, "but I was told kookaburras and koalas are rare out here....." Suddenly, a kookaburra let out its raucous laugh followed by a chorus of others. "Now, are you making fun of me," he cried, "or are you sharing that goddamn swagman's tale?"

******

46

Chapter 10: *LONGREACH AND CHARTERS TOWERS, QUEENSLAND*

At sunset, Dick found a sheltered area to camp and after attending his horse; he lit a fire and boiled the billy. Ravenously, he bit into salt-cured meat with damper, scoffing it down as he turned to Wally. "Hey buddy, this sure is goddamn good and it's a crying shame you can't have any!"

With enough fuel for the fire and rifle by his side, he fell into a deep sleep but was awoken two hours later to blood curdling howls from the scrub nearby. He recalled seeing dingoes near the station and realising they were on the scent for food, he grabbed his gun shooting twice in the air. The dogs took off yelping.

After a few days, he reached town and arriving on dusk, he craved a shave, hot bath and food. He booked into the hotel and stabled his horse. Revived and spruced up, he walked into the crowded bar hoping for the chance to socialise with a pretty gal or meet other cowboys, when he remembered the Australian lingo; gals being sheilas and cowboys, drovers or station hands.

Dick was disappointed by a lack of female company and instead, sat beside a man who quietly introduced himself as Robbie, a drover. They got on well and sat chatting for hours.

Dick's voice becoming louder with each drink, caught the attention of a chap sitting nearby who muttered to his mate, "Yep, he's that bloody Yank who stowed away on the ship I was on." He listened in to their conversation with interest before leaving, casting Dick a sly look.

Dick woke to brilliant weather the next morning and then meeting up with his new pal, he headed to the horse races, placing bets after studying the field.

Suddenly, Robbie nudged Dick, pointing at two young ladies and after eyeing them over, Dick swiftly stated, "I'll take the one in the red dress, you can have the other." He led the way, catching his girl's eye while flashing a charming grin. "Do you pretty gals have a clue as to which horse will win?"

"We just might, but won't be telling you!" teased the girl wearing red.

"Well, I'm Dick and this is my mate, Robbie. You can keep your secret but we'd be mighty glad of your company anyway."

She smiled and turned to her friend. "If they promise to behave, what do you think Dorothy?"

She looked them over replying, "It's okay with me and by the way; my friend's name is Rosie. We're trainee nurses at the hospital."

Dick hooked his arm in Rosie's, and the other two followed suit. They chatted non-stop, pausing only to spur-on their horse which lost, to their cries of disappointment.

Undefeated and assured that *red* was the flavour of the day, Dick announced cheerfully, "I'm going to up the ante and take a chance on that goddamn jockey in red silks!" Recklessly he gambled his last quid and waited anxiously for the race to start.

When it began, his horse held back. Dick bit his lip and with his eyes glued to the beast, intensely urged it on. It appeared doomed as it entered the home straight, but it swung wide as the jockey whipped its flanks. It then began to outpace the others and coming abreast of the leading horse, it nosed past it at the finishing line. The backers shrieked in excitement and after Dick collected, he shared his winnings around.

Later, Robbie and Dorothy left together. Dick put his arm around Rosie, whispering, "I think I could have a fever coming on, so how about a game of doctors and nurses in my room, honey?" Agreeing, she smiled nervously as they quietly slipped into his hotel room. For Rosie, it was a pleasant new experience but for Dick, making love to another young virgin was just one more feather in his cap. Promising to keep in touch but not intending to, he arrived home a few days later where he slept for twelve hours.

He was working in the shed and unaware of the two lawmen arriving on horseback with an extra horse in tow and after dismounting, they approached from behind announcing, "G'day, young lad!"

Startled, Dick jumped.

"Is your name Dick? And did you arrive in Australia recently on a ship at Cairns?"

"Yes," he stammered nervously.

"We're from the Winton Law Office and unless you can show us relevant paperwork, we're taking you back with us to be held as a stowaway and illegal immigrant."

Dick was stunned. He thought he was safe living in the outback. *How did they know?* Then he remembered the man at the bar in Longreach eavesdropping on his private conversation. *Could he be the one who watched me leaving the ship?* Dick admitted he had nothing to show and after apologising to his boss, he gathered his belongings, mounted their waiting horse and rode away.

"When everything's straightened out, you're welcome back here anytime, young mate!" Fred shouted emotionally, "And don't forget - I can vouch for you if you want!"

Dick's gratitude welled up and he released tears, but worrying that his new friends may have informed on him, he begged the Officer, "Sir, how did you know I was a stowaway?"

"A travelling salesman observed you on a ship in Cairns, but you escaped before authorities were notified."

This answer gave Dick a slight feeling of relief.

From Winton, he was sent to Brisbane where the judge offered him a choice; "Either return to America immediately, or, upon turning twenty-one years of age, you must enlist in the Australian Light Horse Infantry. Then,

50

when meeting with the U.S. Military overseas, you will be transferred to them."

Dick chose the second option which allowed for an exciting adventure in the future, plus another year in Australia; even though he had to stay in that area to front-up each week to the local police.

Old Fred was overjoyed by his reappearance at the cattle station and Dick fell into his former routine.

***

The town of Charters Towers is located about three hundred miles, north-east of Winton. In 1871, an Aboriginal boy found a lump of gold-laden quartz and this event spurred a gold rush. By 1917, the town had produced more than twenty-five million pounds in wealth and to the locals, their town was known as 'the world' with all the facilities they would ever need. The town also boasted its own stock exchange - the only one built outside an Australian capital city at that time.

Australians were classed as British subjects then, and with Britain deeply involved in the First World War, many of the young enlisted men were slaughtered or maimed during battle. Others were reluctant to volunteer and with government conscription not yet legal, the number of British soldiers diminished as the war continued.

On ANZAC Day 1917, Dick celebrated his introduction to adulthood at Charter's Towers Gentleman's Club after enlisting in the First World War.

To encourage other young men to enter the Light Horse Regiments and, on being the first American citizen to sign-up in Queensland, he was ordered to dress in full uniform and march down the main street of Charters Towers to its railway station, ready for the long journey to Enoggera training camp in Brisbane.

While the military brass band played American battle tunes of 'Dixie' and 'Yankee Doodle Dandy,' Dick carried out the order with mixed feelings of embarrassment and pride.

He breezed through his training and looked forward to adventure overseas with his own horse Wally.

In six months, that time arrived.

******

Chapter 11: EGYPT 1917 AND 1918

In 1914, there was a strong threat of war erupting in Europe. It was a legacy of nationalism, previous conflicts, complex treaties and alliances, personal ambitions and family jealousies between the world's elite. The spark that finally ignited the horrors of the First World War was the murder of Archduke Ferdinand and his wife Sophie in Sarajevo on 28th June 1914.

The war was in its latter stage when Dick arrived at Port Said, Egypt after disembarking from the steamship, 'Kyarra'. He squinted through the glare of harsh sun towards exotic scenery beyond the docks. Strange cubed, white buildings stood stark among the greenery of date palms, and dark skin people dressed in robes sat perched on top of camels that ambled gracefully along the street.

Suddenly, his entrancement was broken by a voice booming, "All right men, I need your attention! We have forty-five miles to the training camp at Moascar. You must walk your horses in an orderly manner through these main streets before I give the order to mount."

Amid the dust and flies, the men fell in line to begin their long journey; disrupting the locals who watched on with interest as the latest powerful battalion of uniformed men with their Walers passed by. Steeling glances as he walked, Dick eyed women dressed in long drab garbs. "Jeepers," he mumbled disappointedly, "they're dressed like goddamn nuns!"

A sweet scent of incense wafted from a building, drawing his attention to a group of young, giggling females who balancing baskets on shoulders, walked gracefully. His gaze followed one who approached the water well and as she lowered her bucket, he thought she cast him an alluring look through her veil while he stood stunned with deep desire.

Abruptly, he was knocked to the ground by three troopers closely following from behind and they fell like a pile of dominoes. Dick rose swiftly to relish the amusing spectacle but the sergeant turned his head shouting, "Halt!" Humiliated, at the sight of three of his tough brigade lying spread-eagle, he shouted. "You men will be given extra duties when we reach base! Now get your arses up and keep moving!"

"You'll get yours, Yankee!" Dick heard someone sneer from behind.

The tired men settled into training camp, looking forward to their first Middle Eastern meal and although the food smelled appetising, Dick was uncertain as to what it was. He turned to the man nearby, asking, "What are these little white things in our food?"

At last the opportunity arose for this chap to seek revenge yelling, "Struth mate, eat up and don't be such a bloody fuss-pot!" After Dick took a mouthful, the man sniggered, "They're actually maggots but taste delicious and are full of protein." Dick spat it out in disgust; the fellow spluttered a chuckle, then as word spread like wild-fire, the entire regiment's eyes were upon Dick as they erupted in howls of laughter.

After retraining their horses in the new environment, they were ready to fight for British rights to the Holy Land and begin their mission to eventually take the city of Amman in Jordon.

Standing on Israel soil, Dick felt in awe of this place he had read about in the Bible before feelings of regret set in. Shaking his head sadly, he asked his fellow trooper, "Why are we doing this, pal?"

"Cheer up mate!" he replied. "Just think of the excitement to come. We might finally get to kill a few of them enemy bastards!"

The truth hit hard and Dick turned his head in disgust.

They traversed hot open deserts, grassy foothills and valleys, and then a narrow, slippery goat track leading to higher areas but hazardous to climb. The pack horses carried enormous loads and when one lost its footing and broke a leg, it was shot.

"We'll set up base camp here!" the commander shouted, selecting a flat spot. Some men were ordered to build roads and bridges but Dick was given the responsibility of caring for horses and maintaining water supply. He enjoyed this task, allowing him more time with his own horse Wally who was of enormous comfort.

After one hot, mosquito infested night followed by a rushed breakfast of black tea and stale biscuits for dunking, the sergeant shouted, "You troopers have thirty minutes to prepare yourself and horses for action!"

It was a long trek to reach enemy territory and thoughts of excitement and adventure were soon forgotten when confronted by fighters of the Ottoman Empire.

Suddenly, a snipper bullet whizzed past Wally causing him to whinny frightfully. The commander yelled, "Take cover!" The horses were hustled off and the men became engaged in a long battle.

When two Turks ran inside a brick building, Dick's superior shouted, "Dick, throw a grenade in to clear the way and get those bastards!"

After the explosion, he warily entered through dust and debris before stepping into a pool of blood oozing from a mutilated body. When a Turk crawled out from under rubble, he thrust his sword at Dick's thigh. The blade cut through his tough trouser, yet it missed his flesh. Then in one swift reaction, Dick jabbed his bayonet into the man's arm who cried out in pain as he was marched out and handed over.

Feeling a rush of relief, Dick regained Wally from the horse-handler and was about to regroup with his comrades, but before he rode away another sniper appeared swinging his sword. It struck Wally's neck, and both horse and rider toppled to the ground. Rising quickly, Dick found the weapon aimed at his head and in a flash, he thrust his bayonet into the man's ribs, killing him instantly - the dead man's stare remaining embedded in Dick's memory.

He now turned his attention to Wally who lay distressed while dying and in disbelief, Dick collapsed by his side. "No, no. Not you!" he sobbed, caressing his mane before nervously adding, "One day pal, we'll meet again but in a better place than this." He then aimed his rifle and shot him.

Without a horse, his job was to care for the dead and wounded. The stench of death, blood and screams of pain, tore at his being and he shouted to the heavens angrily, "Why such goddamn evil?"

The mud-caked men returned to camp weary and depressed and while Dick sat on the hard ground staring at a peaceful night sky; he wondered why the powers of the universe permit such misery and destruction. Disenchanted by mankind's wickedness, he then fell asleep from exhaustion.

Later, Dick was hospitalised with malaria and an infected foot. Following recovery, his regiment dispersed to other units and Dick was ordered to transfer to American military.

Back at Port Said, he was wiser for his experiences and escaped by stowing away on a ship heading to Australia. Before the vessel docked in Melbourne, he was caught on board and once again, found himself at the mercy of authorities. He feared the penalty of death for desertion yet the General had other ideas, declaring, "It's plain to me that you don't want to return to America and it so happens, you're in luck today!"

Dick gasped in surprise as the powerful man continued, "Because of your particular case, we can't court martial you, and as you swore an Oath of Allegiance to the King of England upon enlisting, I won't assign you to the American military on one condition..."

Dick bent forward engrossed with suspense until the gent added, "You must finish your service to our nation and then you'll be welcome to *apply* for British citizenship."

Reluctantly, Dick complied. Following the war, he was awarded medals but chose to forfeit them.

******

Chapter 12: DICK AND MIN

By 1920, Queensland's sub-tropical capital city of Brisbane held an approximate population of two hundred and six thousand people and their transport included trams and trains. Developed as a river port under British Penal Settlement, it was about seventy miles north from the New South Wales border.

Dick arrived in that town and purchasing a classy motor vehicle offering Chauffeur-driven services, he hoped to break into higher society and seek the company of young women without bothering to seek Australian citizenship.

His azure-blue eyes, tanned completion and inherited suaveness, meant he had no trouble attracting young debutante's at gala balls. But the one who stole his heart was petite and pretty; her nickname was Min and he married her.

They lived with her parents in the city where Dick felt overwhelmed with restrictions and responsibilities of a pregnant wife. He yearned for freedom of the outback and hoping to regain his previous job, he wrote to his former boss Fred at the cattle station near Winton. But the reply stunned him. "Good God!" he muttered in shock. "They say he's dead and the property bankrupt. Now, what will I do?"

"What did you say, Dick?" Min asked.

Preferring to keep his intentions secret, he lied, "Nothing honey; I'm just reading the newspaper out loud." But later, when doing that, he shouted, "Eureka!" A water driller was required to sink bores around the town of Longreach and experienced with that task in the Middle East, he applied with haste.

When a telegram arrived a few days later, he unfolded it declaring happily, "Min, I've got a well-paid, goddamn job!" Then, with a down-cast look, added, "But it's way outside Longreach and only suitable for an unmarried man."

Tears welled in her eyes. "But Dick, I want to be with you!"

"Min, conditions are harsh out there and I have to camp and move around. It would be mighty wise to stay here with your parents, especially in your frail condition....I'll send you money."

"But I love you and I want to *be with you!*" she begged, "I don't care how bad it is!"

He craved his liberty but her devotion hit deep. "Okay then, but don't say you weren't warned."

The long country journey of seven hundred and thirty miles, north-west was exhausting for her and it became worse when he sold his vehicle at Longreach and bought two horses, a wagon and equipment.

Soon, she understood what her husband meant, and although he showed exceptional camping skills, life *was* tough! Preparing food without a kitchen was challenging and the heat was difficult to bear. Their home was a tent and although it was cooler sleeping under the teamster wagon, she longed for a bed but dared not complain.

"Before you become much heavier, I ought to teach you to ride," Dick remarked, watching his wife caressing the horses. Her face lit in excitement and after careful instruction, they set off with a picnic basket to explore the surrounding area.

The idle rhythm of the horse's gait was relaxing, then breaking into a canter through a carpet of wildflowers, they chased a feeding flock of pink and grey galahs away. They circled a hillside dotted by numerous kangaroos before arriving at a tranquil billabong where Dick brewed tea. Enjoying a mouthful of sweetened damper, Min looked lovingly towards her husband. "*Now,* I understand why you prefer this kind of life, Dick."

A rustle of wind blew through the Spinifex and he drew her near but when bending to kiss, he was stunned by a dull peck from behind. He swung around, facing the dumb stare from an emu seeking crumbs from his clothing without fear. Min giggled as he shooed it away and then embracing her, made love.

"I'll never forget this day," she said when they bunked down that night, then gazing at the clear night's sky; she named each constellation until pointing to the Evening Star. "Let's make a secret wish together," she suggested. But that idea was broken by howling dingoes, then as a cold shiver ran through her, she asked, "What if the dogs attack us, Dick?"

"We'll be fine," he replied confidently. "They don't like fire and I have a weapon."

Suddenly, a branch snapped and he grabbed his rifle. Then glimpsing a large shape in the scrub and sniffing a stench, Min clung to her husband.

"Show yourself or I'll fire!" Dick called, concerned it may be human. But there was no reply and aiming in the direction, he pulled the trigger.

Min shrieked as a loud crack pierced the night before her imagination ran wild...."Do you think it could be the Big Hairy Man?" she trembled.

"What goddamn Big Hairy Man?" he asked bewildered.

"My parents had a visitor who told us about it," she began explaining, wide-eyed. "The Aborigines warned him when travelling to Brisbane from Kilcoy and that's where he saw it.... Its half ape, half human and it reeks to high heaven!"

Dick laughed, "I'm mighty sure there is no such thing but to put your mind at rest, I'll check it out in the morning."

At dawn, Min tagged behind as he went searching. He had not gone far, when feigning a reaction of fearful surprise, stuttered, "Jeepers honey, I think I've found your Big Hairy Man!"

Nervously, she drew close peeking warily while Dick stood back chuckling. A large buck kangaroo lay dead on the ground with a bullet-hole in its head, and nearby were the remains of a rotting possum.

"That smaller, smelly animal has been here for a while," Dick remarked, "but I'm mighty sorry for that goddamn buck kangaroo!"

***

The baby's arrival drew near and although they had planned to leave for hospital *a few days* before Min's confinement; *six weeks* before the due date, she was startled by labour pains. Locating her husband, she yelled above the noise from his bore-drilling machine, "I think you should team up the horses, Dick! We need to make that journey now!"

Startled, he shouted, "Are you sure? It's too early. It's a long way to go and I need to finish off this goddamn job!"

"Yes, we have to go now!" she screamed in distress.

"Goddamn it!" he muttered, but within minutes, he had the horses and wagon ready, grabbed requirements and headed off.

While travelling the endless road, Min diverted her mind from agony and fear by focusing on the landscape and although the weather had been kind, storm clouds were gathering. When halfway to town, her pains abated yet she decided to keep quiet. Instead, she imagined resting in a comfortable bed and a change in diet from salt-cured beef and rabbit stew.

At the smell of rain, the sun disappeared then as a clap of thunder boomed, the pains returned gripping her body as they reached hospital. Dick leapt from the cart to grab a wheelchair by the entrance where he escorted her inside.

At that time, men were not permitted into the labour ward. He paced the floor, listening in frustration to her screams. Soon, it was replaced by wails of despair. When another nurse rushed to her aid, a doctor ushered Dick into the room. Their beautiful, tiny baby was lifeless in Min's embrace as she sobbed uncontrollably. Dick held her tight and then succumbing to his own emotions, released his tears.

Grief-stricken, Min dressed the small infant in the Christening gown she had lovingly knit and following a short funeral service, their firstborn son was buried at the town's cemetery.

Their doctor advised Min to reconsider her living arrangements after explaining why their child was too premature. Reluctantly, she agreed to return to the care of her parents in Brisbane.

******

Chapter 13: THE TUCKER BAG INCIDENT

Min yearned for her husband's occasional return and two healthy sons were born at her parent's residence in Brisbane.

Dick arrived home one Christmas Eve and his vehicle towed a horse-float. Min ran to meet him and he scooped her in his arms. "Merry Christmas, honey!" he greeted, "I've brought you and the boys a special friend to keep you company when I'm not around." He opened the door and grabbing the reins of a small horse announced, "I'd like you to meet Black Diamond. She was a circus pony and can do tricks."

Min stroked its nose while gazing into its gentle eyes, replying, "She's gorgeous Dick - I love her already."

He led the pony to the back paddock, explaining, "You know, ever since my Light Horse service; I've enjoyed the thrills of a good jumping horse and that's exactly what she can do. After she's settled with a bit of feed and water, I'll demonstrate but meanwhile, *I've* been hankering for a bit of special attention too."

They headed inside where his two excited young sons awoke from their nap and rushed to greet him. "You may have to take a rain-check on that *special* attention," Min suggested, "I'll prepare lunch instead."

Later, she soon had the pony prancing around the yard jumping barriers. Then her husband warned, "Now get ready for what else she can do when she hears this bell!" Upon that sound, the pony trotted in a circle, bowed gracefully, lay down and rolled over. Min laughed in amazement as her sons cheered.

The following day, her parents held Christmas dinner. Min's brother, Bill, visited and approached Dick. "Hey mate, what's my estranged brother-in-law been up to lately?" Before answering, Bill continued, "It's been a while since you've been home last and my parents have had to help my sister make ends meet."

"Well, it's mighty difficult when the work I specialise in, is way out yonder!" Dick said annoyingly. "And hell, she hasn't complained to me, that I haven't sent her enough money!"

Bill shook his head. "You know that bloody horse won't make up for your company and you should damn well know better!"

"Well, I'll see what I can do, pal," Dick replied, then raising his glass muttered, "Cheers and Merry Christmas!"

Bill was out of town when Dick arrived home for Easter but before he left again, Min pleaded, "We need you *here*, Dick! Please find a house of our own and a job closer."

"Well, I was going to surprise you but I'll let you know now - I've been offered work as a pilot in the outback. I've taken lessons and applied for naturalisation. After I've become a British subject, I'll have my pilot license and more money and then we can buy a house of our own."

Months later, when desperate to inform him of her latest pregnancy, Min's letter was returned and her brother was livid. "My God Min, he doesn't deserve you! I'll soon have that no-good husband of yours found.... I'm a bloody Lieutenant Colonial in the Australian Army, for God sake! He should know better than to test *my* patience!"

Chasing lucrative work contracts between Texas, Boonah and Charleville areas, Dick had proved difficult to track down, but a private investigator soon discovered disturbing news and placed a phone call through to Bill.

"You may want to sit down to hear this!" he began. "He's had a slight change to his name and affairs with two young women. He's wanted by authorities on a charge of bigamy at Boonah and another, for maintenance of a son at Charleville."

Outraged by his behaviour, Bill ordered Dick's return by the date of Min's expected confinement.

When he came home following the birth of their third healthy son, Min was heart-broken. "What's wrong with you Dick?" she asked, disappointed. "Why can't you stay and be a proper father and husband? We still love you, so please try!"

"Honey, I'm sorry for what's happened but I can't live with your parents *or* live in the city and without your company, I'm tempted by other women. After I have citizenship, things will change."

Distrusting him, she began to cry, but he cupped her face in his hands and turning her chin towards him added, "Cheer up honey, I've got an appointment to keep with your brother. He knows people in high places so maybe he can push the process along." He gently kissed her and left.

Bill impatiently paced the floor, yet on Dick's arrival, he called calmly, "Come in mate." Then pushing a glass of strong whiskey into his hand, his tone changed, "We have a lot of catching up to do, so you'll need this bit of *spirit* to last the distance!"

Detecting sarcasm, Dick braced himself for what was to come.

"I understand that military personnel have problems resettling after experiences in the war, but I'll get straight to the point. I've never liked the way you've shunned your responsibilities regarding my sister *and* your sons. And now I've been informed of what your *other* life involves. You've committed adultery with *two* women and *sired two other sons*. Is that true?"

Astounded by his revelation, Dick sank deep into the chair. "Now, who'd go tell you such lies?" he tested with a look of innocence.

Shaking his head at the weak denial, Bill yelled, "Only the best sleuth, this country bloody-well has!"

Totally defeated, Dick hung his head before spluttering, "You know, I do love Min but I can't live in the city and she can't live in the country, so what's a man supposed to do?"

Infuriated, his brother-in-law exploded, "That's no excuse for your behaviour. You are a disgrace to our well-known family's name and we regret that she ever met you!"

These words rang in Dick's ears, and overcome by a feeling of déjà vu, he remembered the story regarding his own pa.... *Goddamn it! I'm just like him.... How strange!*

Bill soon broke the silence, "God knows why, but I know my sister still loves you and a divorce will only bring more shame to our family."

Dick felt a fleeting sense of relief until....

"No! This situation cannot continue! Because of your bad behaviour, you've prevented any chance of naturalisation in *this* State and, I want you out of our lives forever! So I'm giving you *two* options......"

Dick edged closer in suspense.

"I could hand you in to the authorities *now,* and have you sent back to America.... But my sister would never forgive me.... *Or,* I could have you killed," he sneered, "and she would never know!"

Spooked by the last option, Dick's face turned pale.

"God knows, I'd love to do that... but it's illegal. Instead, we'll feign your death and you will disappear from Queensland forever. So now listen, to what you're going to do...."

I'll tell Min that a body was found out west with one of the tucker bags she made for you. She'll identify the bag and believe you're dead, and even though she'll mourn, she'll soon re-marry.... I'll take care of your family until then. Now, listen carefully!

My associates at the Foreign Affairs Department in Darwin are expecting some important documents, hand-delivered and you will be the one to do it. When the papers are safely in their hands, you will receive a generous payment. I'll give you spending money in lieu of my disposal of your vehicle and a one-way ticket on the airplane to Darwin – And I'll make darn sure that you board it!

Meanwhile, I want you to stay two more days while I make arrangements. Spoil your family with attention and when you arrive to drive us both to the airport, bring me your tucker bag."

Dick was eager to leave when stopped.

"Oh, there's more.... My wife and I can't have children of our own." Hesitating, he declared haughtily, "Your second son Billy, *named after me* looks like my side of the family......Once you're presumed dead, I'll ask Min to sign his adoption papers."

Deflated of ego, a tad of sadness crept over Dick while a pang of guilt did too.

Then Bill raised his glass, adding, "Cheers and good, bloody riddance!"   ******

70

Chapter 14: *DICK AND GLADYS,* *WESTERN AUSTRALIA*

Western Australia's first inhabitants were Aborigines who were believed by some, to have lived there for up to seventy-five thousand years. These people survived the country's harsh conditions due to their ancient knowledge of bushcraft and deep spiritual belief in nature's laws.

In common with all Australia's first white settlers, the Western Australian ones were not used to such severe conditions. They endured unimaginable hardship living off mostly infertile and remote, arid land. But by 1930, through sheer resilience and resourcefulness of its people, this State boasted a generous economy derived from production of its minerals, meat, wheat and wool.

The supply of water was paramount to all these industries and, after *leaving Darwin and shrewdly changing his name,* Dick arrived in that part of Australia. Drilling for water, sinking bores and laying pipelines, proved a profitable occupation but three years later, a more lucrative challenge arose.

Contracted to drill for oil in the Kimberley Region, Dick worked with an older man. Soon, they struck it rich before celebrating at the hotel nearby.

"Now we've finished here, mate," his partner began, "why not spend Christmas with me and my family?"

Dick travelled to the southern town of Roebourne following him in his own brand new, Diamond T Model, Ford truck. Meeting for rest breaks, they entertained each other with many tales before his partner mentioned his wife's heritage.

"You know, she's a half-caste Aborigine of the Yindjibarndi tribe from the Pilbara Region."

Intrigued, Dick asked, "How did you meet her?"

"Like most half-caste, she was forced to live on the Mission Station where she was educated to white-man's standards before offered for employment or marriage. She was a good-looking sheila, so I chose to marry her pronto! And I swear mate, I've never regretted it to this day. As for our kids, you wouldn't know they had native blood."

His wife greeted him lovingly while decorating their home for the Yuletide and above the blare of happy carols emitted by gramophone, he announced, "Love, this is my work partner, Dick. He's come for Christmas.... Now where's our pretty daughter, Gladys?"

The aroma of roast chicken wafted from the kitchen accompanied by a cry of distress. "Struth mum, it's only half-baked, so it's going back in the bloody oven!" Taken by surprise, she glanced up embarrassed when her father entered with a good-looking, younger companion.

"Gladys, this is my mate, Dick. He'll be staying for a while."

Her cheeks flushed while offering the visitor an attractive smile.

Dick savoured the last spoonful of plum pudding after scoring the prized silver sixpence. "This sure is the best goddamn Christmas dinner *and* company I've had for a long time," he remarked and then beaming at Gladys, raised his glass of cold beer. "My compliments to the young cook *and* her beauty!"

When the elders retreated for the night, Dick and Gladys played cards while discussing the difference between Australian Aborigines and American Indians.

Struggling between respect to his partner and an innate desire to seduce his appealing, adult daughter, Dick's defence was weakened when she returned from the kitchen offering him a nightcap of cocoa. Sipping her own, cream dripped from her voluptuous mouth and Dick reminisced to his first love, Valencia. He placed his cup aside, slid his arm around Gladys and sensing her enjoyment, kissed her seductively before quietly strolling outside.

When the men returned months later, Gladys' mother ushered her husband aside. Reappearing, he instructed her, "Make us a pot of strong, black tea with a heavy dash of gin, dear!" Then frowning, he turned to Dick. "I hoped you'd ask me first, mate. But it looks like you're going to become my son-in-law. And no doubt about it, you're a bloody fast worker!"

"Well now pal, you've gone and goddamned beat me to it!" he replied, feigning excitement.

The coastal town of Onslow was situated about two hundred and eight miles south of Roebourne and at that time, was renowned for the lucrative industry of exporting wool. Attempting a change of career, Dick travelled with his new wife to that area and it was when living there, he coincidently met up with a distant American cousin, Yankee George. When Gladys gave birth to a son, Dick named *him* George. But Dick soon found the new work unchallenging and with another baby due, the family returned to Gladys' parents at Roebourne.

"You ought to stay here with your mother, Gladys," he advised after their second son was born. "I have to start a new water drilling contract in the outback."

Disappointed, she faced him defiantly, "You're not bloody-well leaving us here without you! I know all about the outback, besides, I can find water and bush tucker where *even you*, can't!"

"Well it looks like your goddamn mind is made up," Dick remarked, adding with a mutter, "God knows why I can't win an argument with a woman."

Following a long journey, Dick stopped his truck beside a shallow creek surrounded by scrubby trees and Gladys sniffed its scent. "It's a bloody good place to set up camp," she agreed before pointing excitedly, "and look, there's also a cave!"

Within one week, a long drought broke and the stream became a rapid. Dick departed to his work site, two miles away and Gladys checked the rabbit traps, gathering bush

74

tucker to supplement their evening meal. It began to rain heavier when she took the children to wash soiled clothing at the fast-flowing stream causing young George to resist. "Don't worry, the rain won't kill you," she consoled, "we'll soon have you dried off by the fire at the cave."

She sat him on a high ledge and placed the baby beside her, grabbing the nappies. Suddenly from upstream, a strong surge of water gushed down, knocking the infant and her into its rapids. Screaming in terror, she swam frantically towards her struggling baby but the powerful current carried them both away. She gasped for breath while fighting to hold her head above water and gurgling helplessly, watched his lifeless form pulled swiftly downstream and out of sight. Depleted of energy, she began to drown when abruptly, she was wedged against a log at the water's edge. She pushed free and regaining strength, dragged herself onto the bank, rasping weakly to God and her ancestors, "Why, why, why!"

When her sobs faded, she heard a strange sound and slowly raising her head, discovered her two-year-old son crouched beside her, sobbing hysterically.

Dick arrived on dusk to find his wife rocking young George clasped tight in her arms while seated beside the fire. Their faces were painted with ash and mesmerised, she chanted mournfully into its dying embers. Unable to arouse her, he searched frantically for their baby and realising he was gone, he lifted his bruised and battered wife to face him shouting, "What has happened?"

When she mutely pointed to the water, he guessed the dreadful truth. "Is he dead?" he nervously stammered. This question shocked Gladys back to reality and following her painful explanation, they cried together. Then, he tilted her chin towards him and looking into her tear stained face, solemnly promised, "I'll find his body, Gladys!"

Their younger son's funeral was held at Roebourne where he was buried in the church cemetery.

******

Chapter 15: *THE KIMBERLEY CATTLE STATION*

Gladys was devoted to her husband and prepared to follow him anywhere, either living in a tent or bough-shed. But one day she was taken by surprise when he arrived home from town announcing cheerfully, "Pack up honey, we're moving north! We now have enough cash for a Cattle Station."

Leasing land in the Kimberley Region between Derby and Broome, Dick bought timber and necessities to improve the buildings before employing an Aboriginal family as help.

He installed a new water tank, repaired the windmill and then shouted to his wife, "Now where do you want that goddamn outhouse?"

"Slow down Dick, or you'll fall off the bloody ladder! You don't have to do it all in one day, now come and drink your tea."

Sweating profusely, he sat impatiently while slurping it down.

"Go slower, or it'll burn your mouth!" she warned.

"You know I can't wait to finish this goddamn place and have it up and running. I'll get young Jacko to work on the chicken coop and pig yard, and Johnno can repair the fence and cattle yards." He then frowned, "So what do you think about that old wood stove? Will it last the distance, Gladys?"

"Bloody oath! It should knock out a few baked dinners. Speaking of that, I forgot to tell you.... There's a new bun in the oven."

A bit slow to comprehend, he sniffed the air, "What are you talking about, honey?" He collected his thoughts and dragging her to his lap, added sadly, "Well, let's hope *this one* lives to grow old with his brother."

After their son Jim was born, Dick's cattle station was thriving and Gladys kept busy milking cows, tending chickens, veggie gardens and caring for family.

Dick was seeking an experienced drover for his expanded herd when a visiting stockman informed him of one in town who had recently completed a very long drive from Queensland. Dick was stunned to learn that his name was Robbie whose description matched that of his old pal.

"That darn God of ours works in mysterious ways," he mumbled to himself, then in the next breath hollered, "Gladys, I'll be leaving for town tomorrow!"

"Why?" she asked curiously.

"I'll let you know when I return."

After arriving in his vehicle, he tracked down Robbie who almost collapsed from shock.

"Geezes mate, what are you doing over here? I thought you disappeared in the war.... Are you a ghost or for real? ....I haven't heard from you since your fancy enlistment party - and what a party that was!" he nudged with a wink.

"Hey, pal!" Dick began in a soft voice, "keep it down. Let's go somewhere quiet and I'll explain."

Bewildered, Robbie followed as Dick informed him of why he had changed his *legal* name.

"Holy shit, mate! I promise your secret is safe with me."

"Now that's straightened out," Dick grinned, "I'll shout my good pal a beer, if you tell me why you're driving cattle over *this* goddamn side of Australia?"

When Dick returned with drinks to their secluded nook, Robbie replied smugly, "I'm a drover, mate, remember? We take mobs from one end to the other!"

"Well, I could sure do with your skills pal, but mine would be a much shorter journey.... I'm now the owner of a Cattle Station," Dick proudly announced, "and although I started with fifty head, it's increased to five hundred. I'll keep a few good breeders but need to sell the rest. Come stay with me and my family and we could work out a deal together."

The pork on the spit dripped as it crackled over the open fire and while their mouths salivated, Dick carved it for the feast. Polishing off with a few beers, they celebrated their success at the station.

Later, Robbie played the mouth-organ during magnificent sunset. Then, beside a roaring fire under a star-filled sky, the Aboriginal family demonstrated a tribal dance before telling tales of The Dreamtime.

They awoke to a glorious dawn and after stoking the fire's embers, Dick prepared a breakfast of home-grown tomato, onion, ham and eggs while Gladys buttered the damper. Then, finishing off with sweet black tea, the men planned Dick's first cattle drive. Robbie did the reckoning; "A round trip covering ten miles a day including our stopover in town, should take less than two weeks - It'll be bonza mate!"

Two days later, Dick geared up his pack horses, farewelled his family, and then through dust and cracking whips, they watched with interest as the two men plus Johnno and Jacko departed with the dogs and herd.

When the cattle settled into a routine pace by afternoon, Dick rode up to lead-drover Robbie who was recalling the young ladies they met at the horse race held in Longreach about twenty-five years earlier. He turned towards Dick grinning, "Geezes mate, you're not much of a lady's man now, all covered in sweat and dust.... but I noticed a heifer back there, givin' you the eye."

Dick snorted, "Well she's not wearing red pal, so she's all yours!"

Continuing to reminisce, Robbie asked, "I wonder what became of those sheila's?"

"I'm sure they're cooking up their husband's dinner right now....and speaking of that; when do we get ours?"

"Well, our horse-tailer and cook have gone ahead. Let's hope they can dish up a good feed," Robbie replied.

Arriving at night camp, Dick pushed a bull aside to wash up in the trough, but the smell wafting from the cook site almost caused him to retch and although mild tempered, he now fumed, "What goddamn poison are you cooking up, Johnno? It smells flyblown!"

"Them dead animal I found left over from a kill - I not waste, boss."

Disgusted Dick roared, "White people don't eat that crap!"

Shaking his head, Johnno broke into a smile explaining, "This for dogs, boss," and then nodding to a pot nearby added, "this ours!"

Later, Robbie retrieved the dog and night-horse. "I'll take young Jacko to teach him the night watch, and then you can take over from one, in the morning," he announced to Dick.

That evening, a storm broke and when Robbie and Jacko arrived for the switch-over drenched, Dick put on his moleskins while Robbie cautioned, "It's over to you now mate, but remember what I said about severe lightning strike!"

No sooner had he uttered the words when dangerous lightning struck nearby, followed by a shake of cracking thunder. Abruptly, the mob began a rush, heading in *their* direction.

"Shit! Forget the camp!" Robbie shouted, "Just get yourselves, dogs and horses into the gully, now!" They looked around for Johnno but he was nowhere to be seen.

The cattle thundered towards them as the terrified men untethered dogs and horses and in the nick of time, they reached safety of the creek. Choking on mud flung from hooves, they watched in relief as the deadly stampede passed, but worried about his father, young Jacko cried, "My big fella dead!"

"Get on your horses and get that bastard mob back under control!" Robbie yelled with no time to look for him.

When the herd settled, the men sifted through remnants of camp, calling for Johnno while his son wailed mournfully. Suddenly, from out of the dark, he walked towards them rubbing bleary eyes in disbelief at the trampled campsite. His son shouted happily, "He here, he here!"

"Where in Geezes name were you when all of Hell, broke loose?" Robbie demanded.

Drowsy and bewildered, he pointed to a huge log. "I sleep in empty tree," he stated innocently. "I keep dry boss."

Erupting in laughter, they began the clean-up.

When less than 5 miles from Derby, Johnno and son were about to ride ahead to set up night camp and unable to find sufficient fresh water for two days, the cattle begun a sudden rush ahead.

Robbie knew by their behaviour, water was near. He warned the men, "Listen up! We don't want the mob trampling each other to get to the soak. We have to herd them into smaller groups and take turns." But arriving at the last with his lot of cattle, he shouted in surprise, "Well I'll be a monkey's testicle! ....This trough is so bloody long; it could've taken the whole mob at once!"

Dick pointed to a signboard. "It says here, it's called 'Myalls Bore' and from 1910, was extended to a depth of one thousand goddamn feet." Highly impressed, he remarked, "Well, I sure ain't dug one that deep, pal!" He then glanced below its windmill adding in awe, "And how about that? There's a goddamn bath-house for the drovers....*Now* I'll be ready for the ladies when we reach town, pal!"

Then, something else caught his eye. He looked across to Johnno, "And here's one for you too, big buddy." Pointing to a giant hollow boab tree, he teased, "If we have more goddamn rain, you won't get wet here either, Johnno!"

******

Chapter 16: *DARWIN 1942, NORTHERN TERRITORY, AUSTRALIA*

Since the end of the First World War, the elite powers of the world continued to squabble over territories, superiorities and assets. By 1st September 1939 Germany had invaded Poland and two days later, Britain and France declared war on Germany. Australia entered the war at that time, following the British lead. When Japan attacked the American Base at Pearl Harbour in December 1941, Australia focused its troops and resources on the Pacific War but two months later, the 'tide turned' when Australia itself, needed protection.

King George V1 was the monarch and Australia's Prime Minister was John Curtin who had previously clashed with British Prime Minister, Winston Churchill. The issue involved a request by Curtin to withdraw the 6th and 7th Division of the AIF from the Middle East to help protect Australia's homeland from an imminent threat of invasion.

Darwin, Australia's Northern Territory capital city was home to a major military base. It was also where Dick had opened a bank account in his *legal* name following payment for the errand he had performed for his ex-brother-in-law, twelve years earlier.

Out of touch to the world's news, Dick had been busy at the station, and although his latest consignment of cattle was sent south, his payment had been deposited into his

Darwin bank account where he intended to collect it, in-person.

He arranged for his wife and two sons to accompany him for a well-deserved holiday, and leaving Johnno and his tribe in charge, they departed for Broome in Dick's truck.

While bouncing through deep furrows created from recent rain, Dick and Gladys were lost in conversation. Young George amused himself, droning monotonously, "Spinifex, Boab, Wattle, 'Roos, Ant-hills, Emus...." Suddenly, his tone changed yelling, "Croc!"

Gladys retrieved the boys from the vehicle's floor after knocking her head against the dashboard scolding, "Bloody hell, Dick! George did warn you!"

More concerned for the safety of the truck, he inspected the result of the thump. "Goddamn it! It *is* a darn Croc!" Then, jumping back on board, he reversed while they all watched in fascination as the reptile crawled away unharmed towards the creek.

Military aircraft flew overhead when the family arrived at the port of Broome. Dick parked his truck under thick cover and paid a local, foreign worker to ferry them to the small steamship waiting at the deep end of the long jetty.

Puffing coal steam from its stack, the loud engine thundered as the family boarded the craft, unnoticed. Dick located the captain who looked surprised. "What are you doin' here, mate?" he shouted, "I'm not supposed to be taking passengers now!"

"But I paid by cheque two months ago," Dick cried bewildered, "so show us our cabin, buddy!"

Mischievously, young Jim crawled out from between Dick's legs causing the captain to jump in fright. "Struth mate!" he exclaimed, "I'm supposed to take supplies up there, not whole families. Things have changed since you booked and I'm surprised you even turned up!"

Before Dick could ask why, the Captain ordered a foreign deckhand to escort them to a cabin while he steered the ship, now running late, from its moorings.

Refreshments were brought to their small room by the same non-English speaking man before the family returned on deck. Dolphins played gleefully, escorting the vessel out to deeper waters of the Indian Ocean and mesmerised by its pristine beauty, Gladys hugged her husband, crying blissfully, "This is bloody beautiful, Dick!" He picked up the children to view the water and agreeing it was a magnificent sight, finally relaxed.

Obsessed by the operation of steamships, Dick explored the vessel from smoke-stack to hull. But frustrated by no communication with the captain, he discussed its function with his wife who patiently pretended to be interested as their sons ran amok on the empty decks.

Seagulls squawked a greeting when the ship arrived in Darwin and eager to be on land, the family took off in haste. But glancing around, Dick uttered worriedly, "I don't like the look of these goddamn war ships, Gladys. When I get the chance, I'll find out what they're up to."

86

He discovered their pre-booked guest-house hidden behind clumps of coconut trees and unable to arouse anyone, placed their luggage inside an unlocked door. The humidity was unbearable so Gladys took the children to the beach. But hankering for cold ale and desperate for an explanation, Dick headed to the hotel.

The idle barman eyed him curiously, "What's brought a civilian to this god-forsaken place, cobber?"

"First, I need a goddamn beer and answer as to why this town is almost deserted?"

"Geezes mate!" he exclaimed, pouring from the tapped keg, "Did you come down in the last shower? They were evacuated!"

"Hell buddy! I've been outback and had no wireless," Dick stammered in shock. "Does this mean we could be attacked?"

"Yep, that's right!"

"Goddamn it! I'm a sure darn fool!"

He gulped down his drink, dashed to the bank, withdrew his money and then sprinted to the beach. He spied his family squealing joyfully in the harbour and he yelled anxiously, "Get out of the goddamn water, now!" But they were delightfully absorbed in their new experience and did not hear him. When repeated louder, Gladys assumed he had spotted a shark and they swiftly obeyed.

No sooner had they gathered, when a squad of aircraft approached. Dick squinted toward the sky. "These are goddamn Jap planes!" he hollered. "We need to take cover, now!" He eyed a rocky outcrop and scooping his elder son in his arms, shouted to his wife, "Follow me!"

Overhead shadows cast an omen of doom and a strange sound pierced the sky. 'Rat-a-tat-tat, rat-a –tat-tat,' echoed from the air and then contacting with rocks, bullets pinged all around in a shower of shrapnel. Dick placed young George in safety before racing back to help his terrified wife who had fallen behind with Jimmy, and while bombs furiously exploded in the distance, they reached cover.

When silence prevailed, Gladys emerged warily with the boys but her husband appeared shell-shocked. Stern-faced, he ignored them as a flash-back from the First World War played out in his mind and then leaving them dumb-founded, he marched ahead towards town.

Distraught by his strange behaviour, Gladys held her sons protectively and choking on acrid smoke, they stumbled their way through streets of burning rubble attempting to catch up. Surrounded by utter ruin and destruction, she pretended a brave smile and then wiping their sooty, tear-stained face, consoled, "We'll be okay sons, I promise." No sooner had she uttered these words, when she witnessed her husband thrown to the side of the road and in horror, held the boys back from fallen power lines howling helplessly, "Dick, are you alright?"

Snapped from his stupor following electric shock, he stumbled to his feet and staring at his smouldering footwear, shook his head in disbelief. "These rubber-sole boots just saved my goddamn life!" he stuttered. With sanity recouped, he led his family to a tattered tree. "Wait here while I check the guest-house," he commanded, but returning shortly, stammered, "It's no longer there."

Suddenly, an air-raid siren broke the silence and the children clutched their parents, squealing in fright again. Outraged, Dick angrily glared at the remains of the government building. "It's a bit late for that; you goddamn fool's!" he shouted, but concerned by a further thought added, "Hell! This could mean another attack!" Through a haze of smoke and dust, he saw the outline of a large drain. Running towards it, the family made it in time as another wave of planes attacked with fury and then deprived of water and sanitation, huddled together throughout the night in dread of what was to come.

They succumbed to sleep by morning before waking to sounds of frenzied activity. "Finally, we've got some goddamn help!" Dick cheered as Red Cross trucks arrived. The streets were cleared and the dead and injured were cared for and then receiving emergency rations, the remainder of civilians were evacuated to the hot inland town of Marble Bar.

Later, they discovered Japanese Forces had also attacked the towns of Katherine and Bachelor in Northern Territory as well as Bowen, Townsville, Mossman and Cape York Peninsula in Queensland, plus other strategic military targets including Exmouth, Broome, Derby, Wyndham and Port Hedland in Western Australia. As well as the ports, many ships were sunk and airfields destroyed.

Many people were killed, injured or made homeless and their towns left ravaged. Controversy surrounded the magnitude of devastation which the Government may have down-played to avoid panic.

Finally, the family were returned from Marble Bar to Broome after its own bombing, and amazed to find his vehicle untouched, Dick lifted Gladys off her feet and swinging her around with happiness, yelled, "We sure are one lucky goddamn family!"

******

Chapter 17: CAMELS AND CHAOS

Following their long absence, the family's unexpected return was a surprise to the Aborigines at the station. Johnno greeted them excitedly, "Boss, Missus, we thought you dead!" He pointed towards the coast. "Big planes make boom, boom sound... We hide in hills from bad spirits... When quiet, we come back."

Dick checked out the area and he was impressed. "Johnno, the station and animals are in mighty fine order. You've done a great job, old buddy! I'll kill a pig tomorrow and we'll celebrate with a feast."

Two days later, Dick announced, "Gladys, we need some urgent goddamn cash!"

"*Now*, what do you have in mind?" she asked warily, rolling her eyes.

"When I drove with Robbie, he suggested that in future, we work for the Cattle Kings. I put a telegram through to him from Marble Bar and it's already organised. Apparently, the government ordered all cattle be sent south for fear of invasion. I'll keep quiet about the rest of mine, but the kings have a few remaining to be taken."

Gladys was disappointed, "Bloody hell, Dick! You mean all the way to Fitzroy Crossing, Halls Creek and down to Wiluna? That's a long way from here and its dangerous territory. We mightn't see you again - you could die!"

"I'll be alright and Robbie's got a good team," Dick reassured.

"We've only just got back and you want to take off again!" she persisted, "how will the boys and I cope without you?"

"You've got Johnno, his women and tribe - you'll be fine, Gladys!"

The next day, she and the boys sadly waved goodbye as Dick set off in his loaded truck to meet up with Robbie and his team.

Summer was over, yet it remained warm. The recent wet season had transformed the terrain into a landscape of beauty. Multi-coloured bush flowers and clumps of green, contrasted vividly beneath red hills and azure blue skies.

Dick located a deep lagoon before dusk, built a fire, and then armed with a weapon, headed quietly towards the billabong. Waterfowl and herons took flight while he scanned the depths. He spied a long silverly shape and watched it linger among sunken tree roots, and then thrusting his spear, yanked his catch out from under pads of waterlily. "I've just caught my first goddamn Barra!" he proudly shouted to himself.

Later, he left his truck at Halls Creek, and with Robbie and his Aboriginal stockmen, embarked on the long drove with five hundred head of cattle, a few extra horses and three pack camels.

A few days later at noon, the scout rode back to Robbie with good news. "Hey boss, good pasture ahead and big trough for cattle!"

"Thanks boy!" Robbie yelled. "Put the billy on when you get there and we'll make night camp early."

Resting happily by the fire, Dick sipped his tea remarking, "Those bovines sure look content tucking into all that green." But his feelings soon changed to fear adding, "Hell Robbie, here comes one of those goddamn whirl-winds!" It sucked up embers from under the billy depositing them above the camp shelter after it had twirled towards them, then fuelled by dead gum leaves lying atop, it swiftly turned into an inferno.

"Shit!" Robbie shouted as they scrambled to gather water. But dashing to help, Dick knocked a native stockman into the fire who screamed in fright. Dick pulled him to the ground and beat out his smouldering trouser leg with his coat.

While the others extinguished the tent fire, Dick returned to the injured man with water. "Sorry old buddy!" he cried after throwing it on the burn. He then applied a clean bandage to his leg, reassuring him, "It'll be right in no time!"

Following three nights, Dick retired to his swag when the dark man limped towards him, handing over what appeared to be two healthy, large maggots. "Boss, you make leg worse," he scowled.

"Hell buddy, then I better look!" Dick worriedly replied, but removing its bandage, he was amazed to find it healed.

The stockman grinned, "Good joke, boss? I make better with crushed witchetty grubs - good for burns!" Then, grabbing back the two from Dick, he threw them in his mouth, gulping them down while rubbing his stomach. "Good for belly too!" he smiled.

After leaving picturesque canyons and gorges, travelling the dry flat area, soon became monotonous. Dick caught up to his partner and pointing to a mirage in the distance teased, "We're almost there pal! I can see the goddamn town from here!"

Bewildered, Robbie strained his eyes. "Struth mate, it's an illusion! Haven't you seen one of them before?"

"Yeah pal, but it's *almost real* and if you stare long enough, you can even make out the goddamn hotel." Then licking his lips in desire added, "I can sure taste their cold beer right now!"

While his pal stared ahead drooling, Dick opened his canteen and threw water over Robbie who wiped the moisture from around his mouth smirking, "I owe you one, you bugger ...But it won't be a bloody beer!" Then looking back at the mirage again, he shouted, "Shit, mate! There are four of them bloody feral camels heading our way!"

Thinking it a pay-back prank, Dick remarked, "That ain't convincing, pal. Surely you can come up with a better one than that."

"No mate, I'm not kidding! Look for yourself... If we don't shoot them bastards, they'll unsettle the herd and our camels will take off with them and all our bloody supplies!"

Dick grabbed the rifle and took off in haste. He aimed his firearm and shot one, but it offered no hindrance as the other randy three, hell-bent with sexual desire, closed in.

Their mob began to rush and Robbie yelled to his men, "Herd the cattle up and settle them away!" He then galloped to assist his camel-handler when his excited, female dromedaries were struggling free.

Dick shot another feral, but the other two remained oblivious and then reloading his weapon, he hit the third as the fourth, now aware of his doom, turned way.

Robbie was still attempting to retrieve his own camels when Dick rode back to his aid. He jumped from his brumby and attempting to calm them, held his arms up to the beasts; turning his head when one spat at his eyes. "Put the ropes up into my hands, pal!" Dick commanded. He then linked them together through metal rings in their nose.

"How come you know so much about these animals, mate?" Robbie asked impressed.

"At least I learnt a few things in that goddamn Middle East!" he replied smugly.

That night while seated around the campfire, Robbie enlightened the men: "You know back in 1860, most camels were brought to this country for the Burke and Wills expedition. We all know how strong those stubborn buggers are and because they go without water for days, they are good for hauling heavy railway and water pipe equipment into the dry outback. But these days with trucks and all - they're not so popular and most camels have been let loose. That's why our country now has the largest number of those wild beasts in the world!"

They broke camp early the next morning and the day seemed endless. Feeling bored and tired by afternoon, Dick complained, "I don't think I was cut out to do this for a living, old pal. Each goddamn day seems like the other. How much longer before we reach town?"

"You've done well mate!" Robbie exclaimed, attempting to raise spirits. "We've only got two days to go.... By the way, did you hear the joke about..." But before ending, his horse whinnied loudly, bucked him off and he fell heavily.

Dick spied a snake rearing aggressively as his pal lay helpless on the ground. He withdrew his whip and at the speed of light, cracked off the reptile's head. While Robbie groaned in pain, Dick assisted him to an early night camp consoling, "At least nothing else appears broken apart from your goddamn arm!" After intoxicating Robbie with rum, Dick pulled his arm straight before applying splints and bandage.

During that night's fire, the Aboriginal stockmen recalled their own snake tales. Dick grabbed the remainder of the rum and like American Indians smoking the peace-pipe; they sat together cross-legged in a circle, polishing it off.

They broke camp the next morning and with Robbie's arm in a sling, completed their long, arduous drove the following day. When cashed up, they enjoyed whatever the quiet, one-horse-town of Wiluna offered before taking off homewards in two overland vehicles to where Dick had left his own.

******

Chapter 18: RESILIENT AND RESOURCEFUL

Gladys' husband had been away for almost six months and with no transport from her isolated cattle station, she, her two boys and dogs had run out of food. They had eaten all their chickens plus the rabbits and birds she had trapped. The meat preserved from the bullock Johnno had slaughtered had been used, and now he had gone walkabout with his tribe. Pangs of hunger gnawed in her stomach too, when her sons asked, "What's for dinner mum?"

It was then, her thoughts turned regrettably to her husband's prized pig. *But Dick will kill me,* raced through her mind and although loving it like a pet, there was no other choice.

Fetching the rifle as tears streamed down her face, she aimed at the sow's head and pulled the trigger. "Oh God, I missed!" she gasped, "and now the poor darling's terrified and has to suffer a slow death." The frightened, squealing animal ran amok while Gladys reloaded and then after a third shot brought it down; she reloaded again, aimed at its head and put it out of its misery.

Although her appetite had disappeared with the botched execution, she was now faced with a larger problem of butchering it. She spied young George hiding in horror, covering his face. "Son, I need you to be a big brave, strong boy. Go find Johnno's old man. He stayed behind when his tribe went walkabout."

Angry at his mum for murdering their pet and terrified *he* may be next, George still cowered only relaxing when she added, "Give him a big friendly smile and ask him to join us for a feast. Take the dogs for protection and let Jimmy ride in the wheel-barrow and be quick."

Usually grumpy, the old aborigine grinned happily as he hobbled towards her but eyeing the bloodbath, he jumped in disgust protesting, "Me too old for big job like that, missus!"

"But we can butcher it together, big fella!" Gladys coerced, almost retching from the stench of blood. "We'll have it prepared in no time and after cooking - it'll be all yum, yum!"

She had already bled the pig with her husband's *best* cut-throat razor while the boys were away, and now with the old man's help, they gutted the beast, throwing entrails to the dogs. A scouring in boiling water softened the skin allowing the removal of bristles. Then, they stuck a steel fence post through its torso and cooked it over a spit, placing the old man's contribution of sweet potatoes into the coals.

The pork dripped and crackled and whiffing its aroma, Gladys rubbed her hands. "It's almost done," she whispered.

Suddenly, her ears tuned to a familiar sound from the distance and although joyful of her husband's return, she yelled urgently, "Boys! Old fella! We better go bush!"

On being a meticulous groomer, Dick was in great desire of a clean shave and hot bath before checking his prized pig. He called to his family, "Gladys! Boys! I'm home! Where are you?"

It seemed very odd - there was no one to greet him and he wondered where they had gone when suddenly, he caught a smell of something delicious. His mouth watered as he was lured towards an animal roasting on the spit.

While his family hid in the bush, they heard the most powerful profanities he had ever uttered. But, Gladys was forgiven and following that day, to ensure the pantry would be restocked, he drove his family into town.

When looking through mail from the post office, he raised an eyebrow remarking, "This one's from an acquaintance at Christmas Creek." Ripping it open his face lit up. "He wants my help at his homestead and for us to join him and his wife there for Christmas."

"Christmas at Christmas Creek, now that sounds very Christmassy," Gladys joked happily. "We won't want to miss that, Dick! The boys and I could do with a change."

He glanced at his young sons, "Well, if you promise to mind your manners and behave, then I'll agree."

Too young to understand, three-year-old Jim glanced up bewildered but seven-year-old George replied eagerly, "Okay!"

After travelling a long way, they reached their destination situated between Fitzroy Crossing and Margaret River

Station. Bearing gifts of beer, rum, Christmas cake and pudding, they were greeted by an elderly couple - Tom, a grey bearded, stern man shook Dick's hand while Joy, a plump, friendly woman, smiled warmly ushering them inside their large home. A brightly decorated tree stood in the corner of the lounge room and the boys dashed feverishly towards candy cane dangling from its twigs. "No boys!" Gladys chided, but they had already pulled off two.

Not impressed, old Tom shook his head but Joy instructed adoringly, "You can have one each now and the rest on Christmas day."

"What do you say boys?" their father prompted.

"Thank you, ma'am," George replied while little Jim muttered, "Ta."

They were happily licking treats, when a strange ticking sound caught their attention. Looking towards the wall, they spied a large grandfather clock and mesmerised; they watched its swinging pendulum in awe when it resonated abruptly with loud, deep chimes. Unleashing ear-piercing squeals causing Tom to plug his ears, the terrified boys dashed to their parent's arms. Then laughingly, Joy then led them to supper.

Later, she played carols on the piano while the boys looked on with amazement. Then, changing its mechanism to pianola while peddling, the youngsters thought it magic as the keys played music without use of any hands.

The next day was Christmas Eve and while Dick helped Tom with repairs, the women prepared the evening feast.

Concerned by no sight of the boys, Gladys checked. "Oh, there you are George," she said locating him on the back step, though Jim was nowhere to be seen.

"Mum, I've been looking for Jimmy and I can't find him anywhere," he uttered distressed.

Instantly, her thoughts flashed back to her second son's death. "Dear God! I hope he hasn't wandered to the bloody dam," she cried out. "I'll head there now George, but you get your dad to follow and be quick!"

She looked everywhere while shouting his name and panicking at no sign of him; threw herself into the dam's depths, searching frantically. Suddenly, her foot became tangled in weed and unable to tug free, she gave into exhaustion. Then gulping while sinking, she sensed a loud splash. Her legs were freed and she was dragged ashore and then pushed on her side, coughed out water. Her blurry eyes met those of her anxious husband, who sighing with relief, helped her to her feet. But recalling her previous fear, she screamed, "What about Jimmy?"

"He's okay," Dick soothed, leading her to a barn. There, she spied his small form sitting cross-legged, entranced by the recent birth of a foal. Accompanied by the older couple, they all witnessed the blessed event together; the nativity, setting a serene atmosphere for that special Yuletide Eve.

Before retiring that night, Tom presented Dick and Gladys with the classic hot cocoa and when cream formed a moustache above Gladys' top lip, the others roared in laughter until Dick gave them a wink, carrying her off to bed.

Ready to depart two days later, they thanked Tom and Joy for their hospitality. Joy replied, "And we are grateful for your visit. Our folk couldn't make it here this year and you filled the void wonderfully!" The family headed homewards while the boys played with their presents of wooden cars and aeroplanes.

After travelling a long way, they made camp before dark. The following morning, their truck started up but refused to move. "Hell no!" Dick yelled in frustration after detecting the cause. "There's sand caught in the wheel bearing and the goddamn thing's burnt out. We'll have to stay put until I get the darn thing fixed!" He unpacked the gear, re-erected the tent, and then using a lean-to-shelter for sun protection, he jacked up the truck. Removing the wheel bearing, he cleaned the hub thoroughly. Next, he replaced his leather trouser belt with cord and with the strap in hand, located his pot of grease.

While busy, his wife announced, "I'll take the boys with me. We'll look for bush tucker but I'll break twigs along the way to mark our trail in case we get lost." She left with a spade and utility knife; her sons carrying a bag and drinking water. They picked seeds, nuts and edible greens and dug for witchetty grubs from the base of Wattle Bush. Piled high with food and tools, she didn't see the reptile until stepping on it. "Bloody hell!" she screamed, dropping her load. But as it dashed to climb a tree, she grabbed the shovel, knocked it to the ground and cut off its head.

"Boys!" she called, "I know you've eaten them before, but what do you call these lizards?"

"Sand Goanna," George replied.

"That's right, but their Aboriginal name is Bungarra, and this big fella will be good for tonight's tucker." Dangling the reptile over her shoulder and loaded with supplies, she returned to camp where she found her husband persevering with his monotonous chore.

After soaking his trouser strap in grease, he continued the task of pulling and stretching it. Overnight, he soaked it again and by morning, re-stretched it to size; Gladys protecting their son's ears when he cursed his disappointment.

"I'll take the boys to find more water," she chirped, "but this time, I'll tie strips of rag onto twigs to mark our trail." They returned during the afternoon, lugging canteens filled with fresh water.

Waiting to greet them, Dick beamed victoriously, "It's all done, Gladys! I greased the hub, wound my belt around the axle and replaced the goddamn wheel. We'll attempt to get it to a workshop in the morning."

The next day, they headed towards home and to prevent the belt from burning out, Dick slowly drove the vehicle seventy miles in first gear.

"We have the parts in stock," the Mechanic announced, "but tell me how the bloody hell, you made it here, mate?"

Dick eyed him casually, "Well pal, all it really took was a bit of goddamn **perseverance, profanity and a pot of grease**."

******

Chapter 19: THE ESCAPE

Dick was feeling restless and in need of a change following the birth of another son. Soon, he announced to Gladys, "Robbie and I've bought a butcher shop down in Roebourne. I'll organise for Johnno to manage the station and support you while I'm gone."

"Well, if that's the case," his wife angrily replied, "then the boys and I are coming too!"

"Gladys, you know your parents don't live there anymore and you need assistance with the children. The tribal women can help you here.... I'll send money and come home as often as possible."

"No Dick!" she insisted. "We've been through that before. We are coming with you!" So, they returned to the town where they had married.

While Dick and his partner set up business, Gladys and boys settled into the attached house and although lacking help, she dared not complain while laboriously attending to her family and new baby's needs.

Dick wore khaki trousers and long white sleeved shirts rolled to the elbows and when home, he expected a clean shirt daily and aiming to please, Gladys did her best for her fastidious husband.

The Sunday dinner was a special event, and the table was set in the proper manner, yet this Sunday seemed an omen of what was to come. Distracted while feeding the baby, she caught the smell of burning meat as smoke drifted from the kitchen. She placed the child down and opening the oven door, discovered the roast dinner had burnt to a crisp. Devastated, she threw it to the dog outside before returning to her screaming infant.

Although her boisterous sons had been playing outside, they now ran into the kitchen. It was then; she heard crockery smash to the floor followed by silence.

Dick was shut away in the bathroom. He was happily singing and oblivious to the chaos outside until he emerged asking, "Honey, where's my clean shirt?"

"Still on the clothesline!" she snapped.

Stepping into the kitchen and onto broken crockery, he gashed his bare foot and it began to bleed. Annoyingly, he eyed the area. "What the hell has happened here?" he hollered, yanking a clean tea-towel to tie his wound.

"The boys are in hiding, so work that one out," she replied, holding back tears.

After he swept up rubble, he threw it in the bin. He then spied the dog gnawing on a large bone. "What the heck is that goddamn animal doing with it already? We haven't eaten yet!"

She announced the bad news while unpegging clothes from the line, but discovering his shirt smeared in bird droppings; she collapsed in his arms sobbing uncontrollably. He patted her shoulder consoling, "It's not the end of the world yet, honey. It could be worse!"

Later, he cooked sausages in the backyard while their sons played happily and then raising his glass of beer to his wife, declared optimistically, "To brighter days ahead!"

Pretending he was an Indian, young George pulled a stick from his back trouser braces and using a fake bow, aimed at younger Jim who quickly retaliated with a shorter stick from his pocket yelling, "Pow, pow!" Faking death, George fell to the ground with eyes rolled back and tongue protruding while his parents howled in laughter.

"I know they love listening to the 'Lone Ranger' on that radio with you Dick, but can't you spare *more time* with them?" Gladys pleaded.

"Yeah well, I may know how to make sons but I ain't a clue what to do with them.... At least they've got *each other* for company."

"But it's not the same Dick! They need your guidance." Then, she thought of a good idea. "If you build them an Indian tepee, I'll make them an Aboriginal Mia-Mia."

The boys excitedly watched with interest as their father constructed their tepee. He placed long branches in a pyramid shape tying them together at the top. Using bed sheets, he held them down over the frame. Then gathering the top, he secured it there and below before leaving an entrance.

The next day, their mother swept ashes from the outdoor fireplace, exposing dry hardened earth. She cut poles from the scrub and tying them together, formed the shape of a small cave. Then covering it with thick, leafy branches, she tied them down with strips of tough grass. Between the two game themes, her sons kept amused while her reward was more time to herself until George ran into the house yelling, "Mum, there's a snake in our Mia-Mia!"

She cautiously inspected the cubby, discovering a curled reptile but as she approached, its head rose, hissing aggressively. She warned, "Stay away boys! It's a desert death adder… Fetch the axe, George!" He returned panting as he dragged the heavy tool.

Sweating from fear she commanded, "Now both of you, keep away!" When the weapon came down, the snake slid aside before rearing up again. Then defiantly staring into its eyes, she axed it in half. Horrified, she watched the decapitated head part, wriggle towards her but she hit again cursing, "Take that, you demon!" Wiping sweat from her brow, she threw its dead carcass into the scrub.

The butcher shop had not begun trade. It was waiting inspection before registration by the authorities and the following day, that time arrived.

The obese man from the Health Department ticked off a list announcing brightly, "Well gentlemen, you have the required experience, the right equipment and the shop is spick and span, therefore I'm happy to have it certified." Laying paperwork on the bench, he placed his over-lapping frame on the stool. "So, to get the ball rolling," he began, "all we need is proof of your identity and your signatures witnessed by the town lawman and you can begin trade immediately."

Abruptly, Dick's face paled at this unexpected request and while Robbie left to retrieve his birth certificate, Dick pretended to search for his own. "I think I've goddamn lost mine," he stammered. "I'm going to need time to find it!"

The man of authority eyed him suspiciously. "You're obviously an American, so a Civilian Identity Card or Naturalisation Papers will do." After Robbie showed his, the gent announced, "I'll go and see what I can work out with an officer regarding your mate." He then left.

This event left Dick unnerved. Even though he was entitled to naturalisation using his original name, he was now using an alias, so his proper identity was useless in *this* part of Australia. "Goddamn it Robbie, I'm in trouble!" he cried in anguish, "You'll have to run this place on your own."

Meanwhile, the astute official approached the head chief at the law office. "I think I may have a case for you regarding an illegal alien."

Before Dick had worked out a plan, a different man appeared on his doorstep, showing credentials. "I'm a representative of the Special Bureau of the C.I.B. and need to ask some questions regarding your citizenship," he announced. Dick gulped nervously as the chap continued, "I need to know where you were born, how you arrived here and how long you've lived in this country."

Attempting to satisfy the man, Dick conjured up a slightly altered story; "Well sir, I arrived at the end of 1915 *in Darwin* on the ship, 'Changsha' from the Philippine

Islands. *That's where I was born and where my American parents owned a pineapple plantation. I've resided in Western Australia since then* and married a woman born in this state. We have three children and I intend to seek naturalization here."

"Why has it taken so long for you to apply?" quizzed the chap.

"I've been working in the outback and unable to do so," he replied.

"In that case, call at the law office by twelve noon tomorrow with proof of your identity and we'll take it from there."

Dick did not waste time in locating his wife, announcing anxiously, "Gladys, we need to start packing and be aboard the boat to Broome, leaving at six o'clock in the morning!"

"Why?" she begged dumb-founded.

"I've been living here illegally. We either go back to the cattle station now, or the authorities will send me to the goddamn Philippine Islands!"

"What about the shop?" she cried out.

"Robbie can't trade without me, so he'll sell up and bring us the remainder of our possessions."

While the authorities investigated Dick's disappearance and background, he and family escaped to their secluded property, waiting anxiously for Robbie's safe return. And three weeks later amid a cloud of dust, their Diamond T Model, Ford truck with loaded trailer, weaved down the track while the boys jumped up and down excitedly yelling, "Uncle Robbie's here!"

Dick greeted him with a hug. "It's great to see you pal, but before we unload the truck, let's have a cold beer while you tell me your news."

"In case I was followed, I left at midnight," he began. "But we did well with the sale. Earned a small profit and it's covered all costs."

"Good on you, Pal!" Dick replied elatedly before adding seriously, "By the way, I think I've found us our new enterprise."

Robbie rolled his eyes with scorn. "I hope it's better than the last one, mate. We don't want a repeat of that again!"

"Look at this, Dick began, spreading out the newspaper; "It says the big guys with big cash are calling for exploration teams to take them deep into the Kimberley."

His partner looked unimpressed. "So how do you propose for us to do that, mate?"

Dick turned to the back page pointing, "Here's your answer pal! The military in Darwin are selling their jeeps and camp equipment from the war, dirt cheap!"

Robbie acted unconvinced. "I dunno mate, I was thinking of going back droving. Besides, how will your missus feel about being left on her own?"

Disappointed by his lack of enthusiasm, Dick urged, "Jeepers pal, she understands my situation and this is the chance of a lifetime! We can afford it and we have a good reference from the bank."

Robbie went quiet before spluttering a laugh, "Struth mate, just kidding. I was convinced from the start."

Dick sighed in relief, explaining, "So although we'll be working in remote areas in *this* State, we'll be *based in another*. I've a bank account in my legal name in Darwin. I'll revert back to that name, obtain my goddamn citizenship there, and rid myself of authorities forever!" Then, he returned with more beer from the ice box and raising their bottles, finalised the plan.

"By the way pal," Dick added, "Gladys is preparing a roast dinner with all the trimmings and a comfortable bed. We hope you'll feel welcome long enough to await the outcome!"

******

Chapter 20: THE KIMBERLEY EXPEDITIONS

The Kimberley Region is a remote and mostly uninhabited wilderness stretching across about one hundred and sixty-four thousand square miles of land in the northern part of Western Australia. This ancient and unique area was believed to be home to the earliest, continuous culture of Aboriginals.

Following the Second World War, the region was about to become wider known and entrepreneurs demanded expeditions to seek the prospective yields from oil and mineral deposits.

Dick's future hung in a balance when he opened the telegram. "Goddamn it, Robbie!" he excitedly shouted, "We're off to Darwin for an interview for that work, closer to the Northern Territory."

The short man with thick dark eyebrows holding paperwork peered over his spectacles. "So, Dick, I see that you've gained all the required skills from your service in the First World War and your partner earned his through years of droving. You're both familiar with the Kimberly area and as the bank has given you an excellent reference, I'm awarding the contract to you both."

After purchasing eighteen ex-military jeeps and all the necessary catering and camping equipment, Dick and Robbie began their new career.

It was now 1946 and Gladys was expecting the arrival of yet, another baby. Her husband was based in Darwin and she had not seen him for months - her loneliness was unbearable. No more cattle were mustered or sold, but she and the boys kept well fed and the station maintained with money Dick sent home regularly.

The Aboriginal women, using their best midwifery skills, aided Gladys during a difficult birth of another son which took forty hours of labour leaving them extremely distressed. Dick arrived home the next day and shocked by their frail condition, held his wife's hand admitting remorsefully, "I'm sorry I wasn't here when you needed me Gladys, but I'm here now and I'm taking you both to hospital for the best of care!"

When they arrived in Broome, it was too late for the baby. The couple mourned for their second infant not meant for this world and it was buried at that town's cemetery.

For the next *two years*, Gladys and her three sons waited anxiously for Dick's visits home each Easter and Christmas. But left on their own following his latest departure, a heavy wet season set in and as like when she lost her second son, the rain was unrelenting. While the natives helped her and her boys escape to the hills, the area experienced a devastating flood, wiping away their buildings and animals.

Dick became deeply concerned when the money he sent home for his family, was returned and he set off quickly to investigate. He was stunned to find the entire station

115

washed away and no sign of life. In panic, he revved the jeep through thick mud, heading up the narrow track that led to higher land. Locating the caves, he spied his old buddy and slightly relieved, shouted, "Johnno are my family with you?"

Surprised by Dick's sudden appearance, he was slow to answer. "No boss, me thought you know - they went big city after big flood."

"Jeepers! But how did they go, Johnno?" he begged, bewildered.

"Big fella from Perth town come in big truck. Your missus cry - she say husband no good. She say no want live here no more. He say your family be okay. He say you get pe'shen and house from gov'ment."

Shattered, Dick flopped onto a log, slowly digesting this unexpected news.

Sensing his loss, Johnno attempted cheerfulness, "You be okay boss - I make billy tea!"

"I could sure do with that, old buddy!"

He sipped the comforting brew, wiping aside a tear. "Well Johnno, this place maybe a long way from Darwin but Perth is way too far.... And if the government is looking after my family and they have a house in the city, then they're better off without me. ....I disappoint the women in my life, and ain't a clue on how to be a good father to my sons."

Dick could think of no other alternative and sadly returned to Darwin leaving the past behind.

116

***

The men stood under a clear blue sky, gazing at steep escarpments and rugged mountain ranges that yielded gorges, thundering with waterfalls spilling and cascading into tranquil rock pools below. Surrounded by boab and grass trees, the pristine environment then led to Pandanus forests and sweeping Savannah. Billabongs teemed with birdlife, attracting crocodiles eager for prey....

"Hey Dick, what's the name of the fancy looking birds at this waterhole?" An inquisitive Geologist asked.

"Well, they're just your average Waterfowl, Cranes and Herons but on the other side, are the mighty Brolgas," he answered proudly.

They watched the big bird's antics in amusement as they danced crooning together seductively. Eager to cool down from the heat and show-off at the same time, the man cried, "If they're having a bloody orgy, then I think I'll join them!" The birds took flight as he dived into the inviting lagoon, when a sly Crocodile raised its head unnoticed, from below.

"Shit, there's a Croc in there, mate!" Robbie yelled, but the chap didn't hear and while Robbie threw rocks to divert the beast's attention, Dick fetched his rifle.

Alerted by gun-shot, the fellow looked up and now aware of his doom, swam frantically to the bank. But with a bullet lodged in its tough hide, the Crocodile only hesitated before continuing towards its unexpected man-tucker. It was lurching for his leg when another slug hit the large reptile between the eyes, killing it instantly. The man dragged himself onto the bank where dripping wet and pale-faced, he feigned braveness, smiling smugly while cheered by the others.

Later, the group was inspecting a deep canyon surrounded by high cliffs of sandstone when one of the prospectors remarked impressively, "This place seems to belong back in the Dinosaur era... And how do we know for certain, if they're *all* extinct?"

Overhearing their conversation from the cavern nearby, Robbie stood tall and with arms outstretched, emerged bellowing loudly causing the men to jump frightfully before laughing.

Afterwards, Dick announced to the fellows, "Now, Robbie and I want to show you something really special!"

They were followed to the entrance of another cave and after the man from the lagoon event, stumbled on a circle of rocks, he complained, "What are these bloody stupid things doing in our way?"

"The native's place them in that manner for their death ceremonies," Dick replied.

"Geezes, this place gives me the creeps!" the fellow cried.

Ignoring him, Dick pointed to strange images on the wall. "These sacred, tall alien figures were drawn thousands of years ago. The natives call them 'Giwon-Giwon,' and were believed to have come from the sky."

"Yeah....Well to me; they're more like ordinary people drawn by school kids," the same man commented.

That night around the campfire Dick explained, "As you've realised by now, the aborigines keep to themselves and don't harm anyone unless they're hurt first. They also believe in a Creator of the world but interpret their story in their own way." He added, "You know, *they only take from the land what they need, to preserve it for future generations.* I'll now explain about the Aboriginal Dreamtime story...."

The same smart-Alec interjected sarcastically, "Yeah mate, bring on the sermon!"

Dick looked across to Robbie whispering, "This goddamn jerk is beginning to shit me off."

"Don't worry mate, I've thought of a great prank to play on *that bloke* tomorrow," Robbie winked mischievously.

The following day, obscenities echoed from a deep gorge as 'the jerk' learnt a hard lesson teaching respect for the laws of nature.

******

Chapter 21: DICK AND CLAIRE

It was 1949 and there were two important events gripping Australian news headlines:

The South Australian town of Woomera, named after an Aboriginal spear-throwing device became the launching site for the country's first air-borne missile, and its surrounding area; the biggest land-based, weapons test range in the western world.

The second event was the commencement of work on the Snowy Mountain Hydro-Electrical and Irrigation Project. A massive enterprise, it was the largest feat ever undertaken in the country designed to eventually supply power to the Australian Capital Territory, New South Wales and Victoria.

It had been three years since Dick's arrival in Darwin and only one, since his and Gladys' separation. He had reverted to his original name and become a legal citizen, and he and Robbie's business venture had made them wealthy.

The partners had returned from the Kimberley Region to Darwin following their latest exploration trip, but Dick was worried about Robbie, unwell with fever. "How are you feeling now, Pal?" he asked.

"Crikey mate, I'm not any better.... I think you better cart me off to the bloody hospital!"

"The gash from the rusty tent peg has turned septic," the doctor announced. "We'll begin treatment, but you'll need to stay here for a while."

"Just get better, old pal," Dick urged before leaving, "And I'll see you tomorrow."

Returning the next day with the newspaper and basket of fruit he asked, "How're you doin', old pal?"

"Not bad for an old bugger." That place called 'Hell' can wait a while... The devil's not getting me yet!"

Reminded of a joke, Dick appeared serious whispering, "Hey Robbie, did you hear about the lawyer who's a patient in the next room?"

Robbie took the bait, cocking his ears, "No; but what about him?"

"Well, he just woke from his operation and because the drapes were closed, asked if it was night already."

"So, what about it?"

"The nurse explained, it's still daylight but because you're a lawyer, we just made it dark for you.... There's a mighty fire across the street and didn't want you to wake up and think you died."

Now realising it a joke, Robbie roared with laughter.

Feeling on a roll, Dick continued, "Did the staff tell you about the Irish priest driving out of Darwin the other day?"

Robbie eyed him cynically, "No, but tell me."

"Well, he was all over the road so the policeman stopped him and noticing an empty wine bottle on the floor, asked if he'd drunk from it. The priest said no, I only drink water. The lawman asked, so why do I smell wine? With that, the priest looked at the bottle crying, Good Lord! He's done it again!"

Dick's charm worked and his pal was chuckling when a mature but attractive ward maid entered, carrying a tray for lunch. Dick looked her over and discovering no wedding band, didn't waste time. He flashed a cheeky grin, "Hey honey, have you got one for me too?"

"It's only for patients, sir," she replied.

"Well, I'm so darn hungry; I could eat a horse and chase its rider!"

"Well, maybe you should chase after that rider," she smiled.

"I'm not only hungry.... I'm lonely with my best pal cooped up here," he persisted. Then sliding towards her, added amorously, "I could sure do with the company of a good looking woman like you *and* opportunity to take you to dinner."

"But I don't even know you, besides.... you sound like one of those smooth-talking Yankees. How could I trust you?"

"Ah, I'm mighty sorry ma'am.... This is my mate, Robbie and I'm known as 'Dick'."

She stifled a rude laugh - the men sniggered - then all three broke into hysterics.

After sharing a great night, the middle-aged couple fell madly in love and married, but there was *one small problem....*

"Don't think for one minute, you can take off without me on one of your expeditions, lover boy!" she warns. "I'm your business partner now too, don't forget - I was only filling in for a friend at that hospital."

Surprised by her strong outburst, he responded casually, "Well... Robbie and I could do with a change, so why not work out a goddamn plan over dinner?"

******

Chapter 22: MISTY VALLEY, BILWON, NORTH QUEENSLAND

By 1950, the tobacco and sugar industry held a lucrative market. Dick, Claire and Robbie leased land on the Atherton Tableland in North Queensland offering the right climate to grow those products and following bumper harvests of high quality produce, the trio made a healthy profit.

Television had not yet been introduced to Queensland and apart from reading books, playing cards or piano; the radio was the most popular form of entertainment and its broadcast consisted of news, music, song and stories.

After retiring from a strenuous day's work, the wireless was turned up loud and listening to an announcement, Robbie could not believe his ears. "You better come and listen to this, mate!" he yelled. "You're the only one with a surname like this in Queensland.... I think it could be one of your many sons!"

When Robbie turned up the volume, Dick heard the re-introduction before collapsing in a chair. "Goddamn it! He was just a babe when I saw him last," he admitted, adding resentfully, "It's been over twenty years since that goddamn brother-in-law of mine forced me to leave my family in Queensland!"

"Crickey mate! That was a pretty good impersonation of Danny Kaye," Robbie remarked before shouting, "Struth, did you hear that? - The host, Dick Fair, has just pronounced him the winner of the 'Amateur Hour' and he'll be heading off soon to the South Coast for a two week holiday."

"I'm mighty proud of him but I wish I could tell him myself," Dick sighed feeling burdened with guilt. He was ashamed of his former irresponsible, promiscuous behaviour and his involvement in the lie to his first family by his ex-brother-in-law who had him banished from Queensland. Also, his first family thought he was dead and he would have to explain.

Unable to sleep that night, he couldn't get them off his mind and although previously a distant thought, he now longed to reunite with his sons and face any demons raised from the past. "Goddamn it Claire!" he exclaimed in the morning, "I'll write to the show's host and ask for my correspondence to be sent on to my son."

Following two weeks, a letter was delivered to Dick. "Well go on, tell me....I know it's from Brisbane but what's in it?" his wife pleaded as he tore open the envelope.

"My son, Rod says he was shocked to receive my letter and though he believed I'd died, he looks forward to a reunion. He's given me his phone number in Brisbane and says; if I can make it to Southport, he'll take me to where the family will be holidaying and he advised me to bring swimming togs..... But that's well over one thousand miles south and this goddamn business needs me here," Dick frowned, unsure.

Understanding his dilemma, Robbie interjected, "I know it sounds creepy but I think the spirits have a hand in *this one,* mate!"

"What do you mean, pal? Spit it out!"

"Well, I just happened to read yesterday about the new flying boat service operating between Cairns and Brisbane and next week, it extends to Southport on the South Coast!"

"That means, if I drive to Cairns, I could make it from there and be back in a few days," Dick remarked happily.

"And don't forget...," Robbie reminded, "we still have your distant cousin, Yankee George to help out before he heads off to Western Australia to cook for the road gangs."

While Dick boarded the plane, he was hit by an anxious thought, *How will I handle any resentment?* But his worries disappeared as the craft gained speed and then lifting into the air, he was overcome by exhilaration.

Late in the afternoon, a young man stood waiting nervously. He had never known his father but had spied a wedding photo hidden deep in a drawer and now wondered why his family was told he died.

When a hand-full of people climbed from the craft, Rod knew it was him. Their eyes locked instantly and greeting with a warm hand-shake, they embraced releasing tears. Stifling emotion, Dick shook his head in awe. "Jeepers son, you're the spitting image of Danny Kaye! No wonder you chose him to impersonate on that show."

126

"It was mum who encouraged our music talents. Our eldest brother, Del can play harmonica, I've acted and sung in theatre, but Billy is a natural concert pianist.... He's studying medicine and can speak in seven languages." He added sadly, "But we rarely see him.... Mum said it broke his heart and hers, when he was adopted by our uncle Bill who's very strict. Poor Billy thought mum didn't love him and never understood why Uncle Bill took him away."

Gulping in shame, Dick tossed his bag into the boot and then seated in the car, was relieved when the subject was changed. "Now tell me about your trip in that exciting sea-plane, Dad!" They chatted all the way to the hotel before Rod said, "Have a good sleep and I'll be back by ten in the morning."

Dick woke early from his top floor room. Drawing aside its drapes, he opened the window and struck by a panorama of ocean, he inhaled its fresh salty air. As the sun warmed his face, his ears tuned into the beat of surf pounding the shore. It was then, he grabbed his swimming trunks.

Seagulls squawked and Dick's feet squeaked as he trudged over dry sand duncs before entering the water. Entranced by the sea, he waded out to deeper surf and dived into its waves. Later, he returned to shower and spruce up before heading to the foyer to await his son.

They arrived at a stately guest-house where colourful geraniums hung from the attic's window box. Dick followed a garden path leading to a shady Verandah surrounding the building with an ornate, open door. Piano music accompanied by muted voices radiated from the parlour where he was ushered to a small group. He felt a nervous twinge when their heads turned and then gathering confidence; he beamed a smile as he walked towards his first wife, Min.

Her gentle eyes held no resentment as he kissed her hand. Now a widow, she introduced the two teenage children from her second marriage. It was then; he spied a young man sitting nearby who looked similar to himself. *It must be my eldest son, I named after my brother,* he thought, but this chap looked away.

"You must be Delmar?" Dick warmly asked, extending his hand.

The fellow now turned his way and declining a hand-shake, his eyes narrowed, "And you must be the father who was once my world but unlike Rod, I was *old enough to remember* and cried with mum when you didn't return!"

"Don't start, Del," his mother warned gracefully. "It's in the past so leave it where it belongs and make the most of the day."

Defying her, he stood to leave. "*We both know why* he deserted us, mum! So, how can you forgive him?"

She ignored him as the younger ones sat puzzled. "He'll be okay," she commented, "just give him time."

All was going well following lunch when Min paused. "Excuse me," she stated before leaving the room. Worried by her abrupt departure, Dick began to panic until she returned handing him a letter, yellowed from age.

"It arrived after you left," she announced, winking mischievously, "I must have known you'd arise from the grave one day, hey!"

Dick's eyes lit up. "It's from my brother in California... I'm mighty glad you kept it so long, Min," he said placing it in his pocket.

Soon, he glanced at his watch scowling, "Goddamn it... It's time to leave.... but it's sure been great meeting with you all." He clasped Min's hand and looking into her brown eyes confessed, "I'm deeply sorry for all the pain I've caused you and the boys."

"You broke my heart and it took a long time to heal," she frowned, "but now you've met with two of your sons; please spend time with them Dick... They still need you!"

"I'll see what I can do... and that's a promise!" he replied.

He looked for Delmar who instantly appeared after eavesdropping. Dick faced him nervously and placing his hand on his shoulder uttered, "Sorry son, I wasn't a good father and for that, I have no excuse... I can only hope you will forgive me one day." He added, "But I'm mighty proud of you and your brothers. Your mother and step-father sure did a good job of raising you and Rod."

Delmar's eyes lowered and he turned away.

While Rod drove him back to the terminal, Dick disclosed *the truth to him* regarding his sordid past.

The reconciliation occupied Dick's entire thoughts during his long journey home. It had stirred many emotions but offered opportunity to front up to *some* of his neglected family. *It had been completely worthwhile - as if the big man above had planned it all,* he thought.

Remembering the old letter; he withdrew it from his pocket and ripped it open.

Dear brother,

It's now June 1930 and although you informed me of your marriage, sad death of your first son, then naming your next after me, I haven't heard from you since. I sure hope all is okay. Please keep in contact!

My vineyard business has made me wealthy and my wife, step-daughter and daughter Marilyn, are doing just fine.

Pa thought you died in the Great War. He's now back at Kansas City, married again and finally settled down. Both younger brothers are studying in Missouri University. Ralph is living in Kansas City and half-brother Leslie, in Saline. Clever guys, huh!

I should mention too, that an attractive young woman named Valencia, tracked me down and asked about you. I informed her of what I knew and although she appeared upset momentarily, she said she was happily married to an Officer in the Merchant Navy with the name of Chad. She had two children with her. It's strange, because the elder one was a boy who reminded me of you....

I'm still your brother, goof head! So please keep in touch.

Yours truly, Delmar

Overwhelmed by more guilt, Dick choked back tears. *That child maybe mine....* he thought, *why did I neglect the ones so close? They should have been my goddamn priority!*

******

Chapter 23: A PROMISE KEPT

Dick scanned the newspaper for an appropriate business closer to his newly acquainted sons. "Claire, Robbie, come look at this!" he exclaimed excitedly. He pointed to the 'For Sale' section coaxing, "Now, ain't that just the goddamn perfect place?"

Situated near the border of New South Wales and Queensland, the rural property included a residence with an attached mail office and telephone exchange.

"Gosh Dick, that's *my* type of business, and look at the picture of that lovely house!" Claire remarked impressively.

Robbie was inspired too. "It says it has a shed and large paddock for livestock and a running creek. Struth, that'll do me, mate!"

Reading further, Dick was totally convinced. "It also states that the Cobb and Co. Coaches fill their tanks from the property's petrol pump. So with that too, we'd be assured of a goddamn healthy income forever!"

They sold their farm in North Queensland for a large profit and moved south to their new home which included a Verandah to cool down from summer's heat, and a fireplace and wood stove to warm themselves from winter chills.

Now a Post Master, Dick enjoyed the freedom of the bush while driving the swanky red and gold, Royal Mail Van delivering mail to scattered rural properties. He became acquainted with the locals and accepting a quick cuppa, he glanced contentedly at the peaceful surroundings. "Now, *this* is the place I want to live out the rest of my goddamn days," he said cheerfully, "and my sons and family will be visiting in the near future."

It was late afternoon and the air turned cold. Robbie was tending the horses when he spied Dick chopping wood for the kitchen stove. "So, what do you think about that cattle sale tomorrow?" he shouted. "All we need is a few heifers and a bull then by crikey; we'll soon have a herd!"

"It sounds good to me, pal!" Dick agreed. "We'll take the dog and horses and then muster them home."

They departed the following morning despite a strong gale blowing and dark cloudy sky. A short distance later, fleeing crows cawed a second warning, when a third was heard - a cracking sound followed by a thump.

"Struth mate, that was close; I nearly wet my bloomin' daks!" Robbie joked. They rode around the large gum branch brought down by the gust and a clap of thunder echoed in the distance. "I hope they don't cancel that bloody sale!" he added worriedly.

"It's just over the next hill, so we'll soon find out," Dick reassured and then catching a strong whiff of cattle, he inhaled it deeply, exclaiming, "Goddamn it! I sure miss that smell!"

Wiping sweat from their brows, they headed straight to the kiosk where they were greeted by other stockmen. After a few icy beers washed down with a good yarn, they inspected the stock. Agreeing on the most suitable, they leaned against the yard rails, waiting for the auction to begin.

The storm had passed, yet the atmosphere was left hot and humid and the cattle, agitated. Suddenly, they were alerted by snorts from an angry bull and watched its nostrils flare as it stamped its feet. Then without provocation, it bounded towards the rail; crashing it open and knocking Dick senseless, to the ground. While the beast's victim lay helpless, it snorted again, lowered its head and charged. Its horn pierced Dick's leg, tossing him in the air before landing on his chest.

Robbie stood stunned.... But before the creature could do more harm, he raised his arms high in the air and with an almighty roar, scared it off. The stockmen secured it in the yard while Robbie attended his injured friend and ripping off his own shirt, he tied the wound, consoling, "Hang in there, mate! - we'll have you fixed up in no time."

The auctioneer telephoned Claire with disturbing news and she was left speechless, but with shaking hands, she plugged the line in to the exchange, alerting ambulance.

Dick was still dazed and in shock. Confused, he asked Robbie repeatedly in a weak voice, "Where did the bull get you, pal?"

Dick arrived at hospital alive and then following days of treatment, he was allowed home but with strict instructions to rest - a difficult task for one, so energetic. Bearing a broken rib and injured leg, he longed to return to his duties, watching helplessly as Robbie and Claire carried out the extra workload.

"You've been a great pal, Robbie," Dick announced with gratitude. "And you goddamn saved my life too! How can I ever make it up to you?"

Robbie smirked deviously, "By making friends with that big bastard of a bull who's now part of our family!"

Interpreting his answer as a joke, Dick calmly played along.... "So, you bought him after all?"

"Yep mate!" Robbie replied seriously, "It was while I was with you at the hospital. The auctioneer rang for our bid, and now that big beast himself, is in our own bloody paddock going hell for leather with those pretty heifers!"

Dick was gob-smacked and when Claire spluttered a chuckle from the other room, he yelled her way, "When I'm healed; that goddamn bull might have competition of our own!"

"What a *load of bull*!" she replied.

The men were laughing until Dick cried out in pain, "Jeepers Claire, I think I've just cracked another rib!" But when she approached to check, he grabbed her arm and pulling her to his lap, his gammy leg gave way and she fell undignified to the floor.

"Blimey mate!" she scolded. "You were put out to pasture, don't forget!"

"But not forever, honey," he warned, winking amorously.

Robbie looked at them both in disgust. "Struth, I'm out of here! - I'll go watch the bull and heifers instead."

Dick read everything available and talked incessantly on the phone but early next day, his wife chirped, "Your sons have arrived with their families!"

"Bloody hell dad, why didn't you tell us you were injured?" Rod asked.

"Yeah, if we knew," Del added, "we could have left the family at home and helped you out."

"But that's the reason why I kept quiet - I want to meet my grandkids."

When one young boy and two younger girls entered the room with their mums, Dick was surrounded with love.

Del watched his father's enjoyment of his own wife and two children as he handed him a cup of tea, and then sitting by his side, whispered.... "I forgive you dad."

Dick smiled and patting Del's arm choked, "Thank you son; that means the world to me."

When the families departed late afternoon, Dick gazed fondly at Claire. "I'm mighty thankful you hosted the family, honey.... I don't know what I'd do without you."

"Oh yes you would," she teased. "I saw you smooth-talking your daughter-in-law's. You can have any female you want, eating out of *your* hands!"

"But I love *you,* Claire," he smiled and clasping hers, kissed them tenderly.

Alone the next day, he sat under the apple tree reviewing his life and thinking about his sons. Apart from the first who died as an infant, he had sired another three to Min, plus the two he knew about from his affairs in Queensland. And, together with his wife Gladys in Western Australia, he had two who died as infants but three who survived. He wondered how many other children may have been born as a result of his irresponsible behaviour and in what way, his absence may have affected them all....*And what would their families endure*, he now thought, *if they were deserted by them?*

His thoughts drifted again to Gladys living on the other side of the country.... *She had been a good wife and mother with remarkable qualities of resilience and that family endured a difficult life.... Were they happy, and still living in Perth?*

"Goddamn it, I've been a fool!" he mutters and remorsefully searches memory for words preached at his first marriage to Min.....

"Dick, where are you?" Claire called. She discovered him looking towards heaven, seated comfortably in a cane chair. "Are you receiving a message from God?" she taunted.

Suddenly recalling the words preached by the Minister at his first wedding, Dick mumbled, "Health is the greatest gift, contentment, the greatest wealth, and *faithfulness,* the best relationship."

"Wow! That sounds nice, Dick. But now you're talking to yourself - I'm worried you're going nuts!"

Jolted to the present, he smirked, "Well then, I ought to hide that goddamn rifle of mine before you get any bright ideas." She kissed him on the cheek; he steadied himself by her side and together, walked back to the house.

Now fully recovered, he was tending to the work he loved while relishing each moment, but little did he know his God had only given him a *short reprieve.*

He awoke from sleep moaning, "It's too painful to move and I feel crushed."

"Good Lord! It's a heart-attack!" Claire cried, scrambling to the switchboard....

Months had passed since the incident with the bull when Dick took his last breath on that journey to hospital, and then pronounced dead at Tenterfield, New South Wales, he was later buried across the border in the Returned Soldiers Section of Stanthorpe's Cemetery.

Continued....

EPILOGUE

It was during the year of 2001 when Dick's son Jim, from the Western Australian family, stumbled across internet information regarding his dad's other life in Queensland.

Jim discovered he had half-brothers to Dick and his first wife Min, but they were no longer living. Then, through a contact address, he discovered a half-brother who was alive and they met.

Mervyn was an innocent third person, born from an affair Dick had with a young Governess at a cattle station near Charleville. He was later adopted out. It was one of the two extra-marital relationships Dick had, spurring the Tucker Bag story's creation by his brother-in-law. It had caused Dick's wife to believe her husband had died out west, when in fact was banished from that State by her powerful brother. Jim finally knew the 'Tucker Bag Incident' was true.

When told about the sad death of his father in 1953 and the location of his grave, he understood the strange feeling of connection he had experienced many years ago passing through the town of Stanthorpe – his father's body had been buried in that town's graveyard.

Jim; who lived an adventurous life himself, chose to live out his retirement in the U.S.A. where he died in 2013. At 'Aussie Jim's' funeral service; American Military Ex-servicemen performed full military honours for his active

service in the Australian Army during the Malayan and
Vietnam Wars.

******

www.ingramcontent.com/pod-product-compliance
Lightning Source LLC
Chambersburg PA
CBHW052105090426
42741CB00009B/1685

9 780099 442002